REFLECTIONS OF A TRAVELING SCHOLAR

by

CLIFFORD HALLAM

First published by Dog Ear Publishing
4011 Vincennes Rd
Indianapolis, IN 46268
www.dogearpublishing.net

ISBN: 978-1-4575-4330-2

This book is printed on acid-free paper.

Printed in the United States of America

In memory of my parents, who kept faith in me, and with gratitude to my family, friends, and colleagues, whose encouragement, friendship, and love made possible these fragments I have shored against my ruins.

CONTENTS

Introduction

It is a melancholy of mine own, compounded of many simples, extracted from many objects, and indeed the sundry contemplation of my travels, which, by often rumination, wraps me in a most humorous sadness.— Shakespeare

Shortly after WWII, while still in grammar school, I marched with my classmates single file to the auditorium each Friday afternoon for assembly. Invariably, we would watch a travel film featuring an idyllic country far removed from my Norman-Rockwell-cover hometown in Closter, New Jersey. The footage never included a single negative image: no sign of poverty, disease, or civil unrest, much less outright rebellion, revolution, or insurrection—the triple response to misery, discontent, and oppression throughout the world. The narrator, whose tone and diction resembled an American Ronald Colman, would typically close with the phrase: "And now we say goodbye to our happy island. . ."

I was mesmerized, stunned, enchanted by those exotic scenes. Although transfixed by movies such as *Snow White, Fantasia, Bambi,* and similar Disney productions foregrounding American fantasy, I understood, vaguely, the difference between the cartoon prism and photographic likeness: the presumed "real." Thus, I trusted implicitly the genuine, wide-awake vision of graceful palm trees, sublime ruins, picture-perfect deserts, jungles, waterfalls, and mountain ranges. These natural wonders offered a bonus: a land of Oz, populated by people of various non-white hues in costume-party array, always smiling or laughing, frolicking in the emerald waves, dancing in thatched villages, waving frantically—not so much to an imagined audience, but directly at their special American friend: me. While pacing out of the auditorium to the strains of "Marching to Pretoria," I made a silent vow: *Someday I'll go there.*

And I did, with a vengeance—but not as a tourist. True, in 1966 I took the Grand Tour shortly after earning an MA at Northeastern. With my acceptance to the graduate program at the University of Illinois, first visiting various European cultures helped prepare me for advanced courses in literature, criticism, and linguistics. Moreover, I brushed up on two or three foreign languages, which required considerable burnishing. Some twenty years after war, however, countries like Sweden, Germany, France, and Italy had largely lost their exotic flavor. Typically, native speakers throughout the Continent also spoke fluent English, particularly at hotels, restaurants, and popular sites. Throughout the summer of 1966, I visited some fifteen different countries, and I was never at a loss, owing to that fact that I only spoke English with considerable skill.

Moreover, as a student of Western culture, I often felt a sense of déjà vu when visiting museums, cathedrals, ruins, and celebrated cities like London, Rome, and Paris. Upon returning to the States in August 1966, I remained homebound until 1980, when I departed for locations more in keeping with the truly exotic "happy islands" of the travel films: Saudi Arabia, Thailand, Turkey, North Cyprus, Poland, and Belarus. I also traveled throughout the Middle East, speaking functional Arabic, and made forays into Austria, Russia, Spain, Syria— no longer an innocent abroad, but a seasoned traveler whose well-stamped passport bulged like a Texas roll.

Recently divorced and shortly before leaving to Riyadh, the capital of Saudi Arabia (which I could barely locate on the map), I met a young woman whose intelligence, humor, and charm reminded me of Dr. Johnson's observation about a second marriage: "The triumph of hope over experience." I told Monica that I had signed a letter of intent, not legally binding, but still a matter of *noblesse oblige*, since I was then and still am a man of my word. She understood, but decided to cast the *I Ching*, in the belief that Oriental divination might point the Way. By an unlikely and disturbing coincidence, the yarrow sticks indicated the exact hexagram: traveling scholar. Thus, by Jungian synchronicity or kismet, one embraces his destiny foretold: in Arabic, the phrase *"maktoob"* [it is written] says it all.

I spent nearly twenty-five years overseas until my retirement in 2004 at age sixty-five. Unlike most young Americans on a professional track, my career abroad conformed to no calculated plan. Indeed, my long sojourn in third-world countries was thrust upon me: no immediate employment after almost two decades at the podium and no prospects, though not for lack of effort, in the United States. I sometimes felt like a lone wolf in search of food and shelter; each time I awoke, it was a new day. For nearly two and a half decades, I measured time in brief units. Except for Thailand, where I lived from 1983 until 1989, a three-year time span was the limit, often less.

Various reasons, ranging from emotional exhaustion (Saudi) to utter disgust with the anti-Semitism (Poland), prodded me to resign and move on to greener pastures. Thus during my exile, I lived and worked in seven different countries, some alike (Turkey and Northern Cyprus) and others radically different (Saudi and Thailand). But each post required considerable adjustment, beginning with basic communication and often confronting/braving a national language far removed from the Indo-European tree. As a college student, I studied and sometimes passed exams in Spanish, German, and French. English is a Germanic tongue, and the loan words from Romance languages (especially the Gallic influence) are legion. Arabic, Thai, and Russian require learning a radically different phonetic system. To converse in the Middle East with minimal efficiency means attempting, though never mastering after a certain age, tongue-twisting phonemes. A native Thai speaker fails to understand homophones of common words like "small" and "iron" when lacking the proper tone, five in total, so each phrase is likely to require the full range.

As a middle-aged liberal trained in the humanities, the entrenched notion of cultural relativism was soon put to the existential test. Certain quaint customs—eating without utensils but only with the right hand, removing one's shoes before entering a household, or nodding left and right to mean "yes"—posed no personal challenge beyond an occasional awkward moment: a matter of remembering social rules and the semiotics of local protocols. Matters of ethical import, however, proved a great deal more complex. Throughout the Orient, for example, at every level starting at customs, bribery allows one to negotiate the double binds of bureaucracy. I once witnessed a soldier at the

Bangkok airport accept a bottle of Scotch; he then marked an unopened suitcase with chalk, the sign of clearance. None of the other passengers/functionaries took notice.

In Thailand I knew a Welch-born security officer at the British embassy. He was charged by the government to investigate the practice of corruption among UK citizens. For weeks Ian failed to arrive at the office on time, owing to morning gridlock on the side street where he lived. The officer held his hand, palm forward, for an unconscionable time, thus preventing the *"farang"* [foreigner] from entering the main road leading to his office. An old hand made a suggestion: offer the soldier directing traffic a bottle of whisky. Ian, although basically honest, appreciated the irony. Yet he also understood the pragmatics of employment, since his chronic tardiness did not go unnoticed at the head office. Eventually, Ian purchased a fifth of Mekong, the local guaranteed hangover, along with a vendor snack for good measure, and smiling broadly, he approached the traffic officer bearing gifts in the approved Oriental manner. Afterward, he arrived each morning at 9:00 sharp, ready for work.

One year, my renewable visa application, ordinarily a *pro forma* procedure, turned up "lost" at the immigration office. I made several trips, which were time-consuming and a waste of cab fare. After the deadline passed, I was technically an illegal immigrant. Consequently, I might have been arrested, jailed, fined, and deported. An American colleague, whose worldly wisdom exceeded his slender cosmopolitan experience, offered advice in parental tones: "Just go along with the program. You are a guest, and it's their culture." I found the argument disingenuous. I had a culture, too. And no matter how widely practiced, corruption was illegal. If I were arrested for bribing a government official, no magistrate would countenance the "everyone does it" defense. Moreover, as a colleague at the Riyadh University observed, "Where's the cultural relativism in the universal disposition to misrepresentation?"

To date, I have yet to meet anyone, no matter how depraved, eccentric, or removed from democratic principles, who enjoys being cheated. As for Thai understanding of irregular practices, actual or imagined, when a Chulalongkorn professor of archeology discovered a "missing" lintel in an American museum, the entire country affected outrage. An image of the vanished Vishnu appeared on public buses, and government buildings were festooned with posters demanding the artifact's return. Sale and export documents in good order did not satisfy national pride, so the Chicago museum returned the missing lintel without charge.

During my sojourn overseas lasting two and one half decades and including posts in seven different countries, I held that obeying the law was not only right, but good policy. I represented America, my profession, and most importantly my own sense of worth. Since I never engaged in criminal activities (save black-market currency exchanges in Minsk), however, local regulations rarely affected my decisions or behavior. Consequently, I conducted myself outside the classroom in a law-abiding manner, like the Zen pilgrim who lives in but not of the world—except no such refuge from ethical decisions exists.

Throughout my career in both the United States and abroad, academic dishonesty regularly confounded attempts to teach effectively—social class, university prestige, or any other variables notwithstanding. Student scandals occur at Harvard, Yale, and the military academies; no institution is exempt.

The response, however, to the chronic problem of cheating varies. In Saudi, for example, plagiarism was often overlooked owing to the fact that the native instructors themselves had rarely earned advanced degrees in legitimate fashion. As the comedian Chris Rock observed, "I'm not saying that OJ should have killed his wife and her lover. But I *understand!*" Arabic speakers in concert with foreign faculty members patrolled final exams. Those who used crib notes, whispered among themselves, or gazed on a fellow student's answer sheet were summarily expelled from the "Control Room" and failed the course. No one, to my knowledge, was suspended from school.

Turkish students consider copying exam answers, plagiarism, and generally manipulating the grading protocols as simply part of the education process. In fact, the sons and daughters of the Ottoman rulers typically cheat their way through school. Atypically, the private university where I taught required no entrance exam. Tuition was prohibitively high, except for the wealthy. Ergo, those who paid for their education demanded a degree in any subject, including medicine, law, and engineering. As for the arduous process, "ends justify the means"—perhaps the most repeated rationalization on record.

When caught *en flagrante delicto*, the young scholars under my direction reacted with barely concealed outrage for the inconvenience. A satisfactory remedy, however, was at hand: a rewrite in the case of outside assignments or a retake for unacceptable exams. A committee "set up" (in both senses) by the Chair took it upon themselves to grade the second-chance effort. "Fair enough," the administrators reasoned, in order to prevent any charge of revenge, incompetence, or unfairness on the part of the martinet who had taught the course. Yet everyone passed eventually, no exceptions save once, although the seniors who failed a required survey in English literature under my direction might have been graduated that spring. I never enquired. Some matters, regardless of personal interest, are beneath contempt.

Owing to my refusal to issue a make-up exam, the dean cancelled my two-year contract without explanation or a hearing. On the advice of a Cypriot colleague, I then applied for a post at Födz University, where I taught graduate seminars, after summer school, for less than two full terms. After the Chair and dean at FU tendered an equal number of insults nicely complementing egregious professional injuries, I left in late spring minus $6000 USD in unpaid salary. Back in America, during a conversation with a former colleague, I stated, "Don, high dudgeon can be very expensive." No stranger to office politics, he replied, "It always was."

Lukashenko, the Belarusian dictator, admired Stalin tactics. When I served as the American Fulbright Scholar (1998–99), he ran for election with three political opponents. One died unexpectedly; another was arrested and jailed. The third fled the country, living in exile. The good citizens imprinted by communism followed, like sheep, their leader's example. Although careful to obey draconian rules according to social/political doctrine, the authorities broke established university conventions with impunity. Thus, cheating went unpunished, chronic absenteeism mattered little, and corruption informed all aspects of the failed system. I presided over oral exams like a scene from Beckett's *Endgame*. In response to direct questions on literary history/texts, the young scholars responded sullenly with *non sequiturs* or played deaf. Checking an MA thesis against Harold Bloom's *The Western Canon*, I found passages copied verbatim. An Ethiopian student, studying Russian at the Minsk State Linguistic University, openly handed the dean a television that was worth a year's salary in rubles. He received, but did not earn, a diploma.

Although invited to return for a second year, I resigned shortly after arriving safely in the States, where I retired.

The chapters that follow, then, roughly follow the linked topics of travel and teaching. Structurally, the text is divided: part I focuses on teaching/scholarship, while part II addresses several junkets in detail. Despite the aggrieved or sarcastic tone of the persona in some passages, I loved every minute of my overseas adventures, which were informed by memorable meals, exotic customs, fascinating trips, unforgettable students/colleagues, and lifelong friendships. I often felt guilty about accepting the predictable meager salary (in most instances) for my services/duties, which were rarely onerous in any case. Like Socrates, I would have gladly held forth *gratis* and gratefully—if only I could have afforded the pleasure.

. . . .

Students of literature are often asked to name a favorite title, genre, seminar topic, and so on. After such question, what sensible answer? No one has yet asked me to name my favorite character, but I have a reply: Dr. Charles Kinbote, Russian/French speaking scholar, prince in exile, homosexual, and paranoid schizophrenic suffering from delusions of persecution and grandeur. He is also the controlling voice of Nabokov's *Pale Fire*. I answer to none of the above identities/traits. Yet counter-intuitively, the novel's radically ambiguous narrator, who cannot be identified with certainty, earns my heartfelt sympathy. He is also a devout Catholic, which faith does not resonate with me—though in a secular manner, I endorse Christian virtues including charity and the Corporal Works of Mercy.

As for Kinbote, I believe that one casual statement in passing earns him, despite a number of disagreeable mannerisms and questionable behavior, redemption. During his highly imaginative interpretation, which bears almost no resemblance to the poem under analysis, Charles the Beloved (his delusional self) makes a surprising statement, given the fact that his colleagues/neighbors reject and ridicule the tormented scholar who finds himself a stranger in a strange land. In his wrong-headed, personalized, absurd "scholarly" commentary on "Pale Fire," he quotes a vicious insult. Sybil Shade, the poet's wife, holds no sympathy for the narrator, an eccentric neighbor who pesters her husband and imposes himself on her grudging hospitality. She is, according to bourgeois protocols, just barely civil to his face. Yet in typical fashion she talks behind his back.

Professor Kinbote reports that, although "... I tried to behave with the utmost courtesy toward my friend's wife, she disliked and distrusted me. I was to learn later that when alluding to me in public she used to call me 'an elephantine tick; a king-sized botfly; a macaco worm; the monstrous parasite of a genius.' I pardon her—her and everybody."

And so do I.

I.

The Perfect System

DOUBLETHINK means the power of holding two contradictory beliefs in one's mind simultaneously, and accepting both of them.— Orwell, *1984*

After dark, when the dreamlike moon, chalk-white or saffron yellow or rose red, palely illuminated the empty quarter to the west of Riyadh, the capital of Saudi Arabia, the Khazan Street *souq*, lit fitfully by yellow neon tubes, glowed like a dying star. Inside the building, which smelled of incense, scores of tables heaped with every imaginable item ranging from fresh fruit to prayer rugs, from vegetable cookers to golden trinkets, brought to life a Rembrandt painting—magical patterns of light and shadow, a Renaissance still life in *chiaroscuro*. Rich in texture, the evening tableau offered a model of Oriental fantasia, which mirrored both the natural and social environment. Life in the Perfect System remained empirically substantial, but simultaneously amorphous: unpredictable, unreliable, and uncertain. Noting the Disney-like atmosphere, foreign experts, who essentially ran the country "off camera," renamed Saudi Arabia the "Magic Kingdom."

One soft winter evening while browsing among the profusion of imported goods from near and far—Jordan, Yemen, Iran, Europe, and the United States—an elfin *bedu* wrapped in a camel-hair blanket against the chill turned as I approached, and he beamed, eyes glinting like black buttons. He stood at the copperware stall, where the desert dweller was bargaining over a coffee pot covered in Kufic script. At the greeting, he spread his arms wide and embraced me tightly. "*Ahlan wa sahlan* [Welcome, most welcome]," he said. "*Al humdilillah* [Allah be praised]," I replied, returning his brotherly hug with firm pats to his narrow, bony shoulders. I released him and stood back. "*Hayakallah* [Go with God]," he rasped. I replied, "*Tisbu allah khaier* [May you have a good morning]," and made my way to the exit.

I felt giddy with surprise. I knew from countless public encounters off campus at King Saud University, where I taught literature and related subjects to a very few graduating seniors, that xenophobia, especially regarding unbelievers, often trumped hospitality. The stern, ubiquitous religious police, wearing a full beard dyed with henna and carrying a thick staff to bang sharply on metal store shutters and prod sluggards into the mosque, did not tolerate foreigners. Indeed, the *mataween* usually glared by way of response to the salutation: "Peace be unto you." Thus, the unexpected warm welcome by a desert sheik proved a watershed moment. Bigotry certainly obtained in Riyadh, but exceptions—though rare—occurred. I returned to my apartment on foot, with a skip in every step.

Only a few months after my arrival in Jeddah ("The Grandmother's" (Eve) resting place) in 1980 before the short hop to Riyadh [city of gardens], I came to appreciate the Darwinian phrase "survival of the fittest" was better understood, not in terms of strength and aggression, but rather one's capacity to adapt. The first wise move: learn some functional Arabic. Consequently, I purchased texts, listened to tapes, hired a tutor and, in 1981, attended the famous Riyadh Arabic Language Institute, located only a short walk from my apartment. An earnest attempt to communicate with the natives, to read newspaper headlines, short notices, and street signs earned me unexpected status in the community.

Native speakers readily forgive poor pronunciation, tortured syntax, impossible predication, and even logical lapses in lively conversation. The effort to speak with locals on equal terms is considered more than sufficient, and the tongue-tied speaker's native interlocutor makes known his appreciation. One boiling hot afternoon, while waiting in an endless line to change my plane ticket, a clerk grasped my arm and led me to the airport official's window, while my less-fortunate monolingual colleagues grumbled in protest. The word had spread throughout the campus: "*Ustādh Hallam yatākallum al-loirabia mathal al-bulbul* [Professor Hallam speaks Arabic like the nightingale]." That comparison, a feeble joke, made the rounds, but hyperbole was not unknown in the Najdi dialect, so I gratefully accepted the undeserved compliment.

In public I sometimes attracted, like a dancing bear, admirers of my bourgeoning linguistic talents. Typically, after exchanging a few phrases (mostly memorized on my part), the native speaker would shout, "Abdullah, look! He speaks the Arabic language well." Soon several young men in spotless *thobes* would surround me, like children in the schoolyard, and ply me with questions: country of origin, home state, purpose in Riyadh, number of sons, and similar enquiries. I quickly learned the routine and provided the appropriate answers. Inevitably, by way of closing the command performance, one would shout in English, "Welcome to my country!"

Despite those privileged moments, which occurred on a regular basis during my three-year stay in Saudi Arabia, the oil-rich country was a theocratic police state, where petty rules were strictly enforced and applied, arbitrarily, by virtually all male citizens: soldiers, police (religious and secular), bureaucrats, and even schoolboys in military uniform. Living in Riyadh was an exercise in paranoia. A colleague was summarily fired when a disgruntled undergraduate reported, "Dr. Terry cursed Islam!" Certainly, no one publically downgraded the official religion in the peninsula, period. Quite likely, such an outrage would have resulted in a public lynching—or a serious attempt.

To describe without irony the government, culture, and ethos of Saudi Arabia as the "Perfect System" would be ludicrous, like defining the sun as a cold, black will o' the wisp. Oil money greases the grinding wheels of the social infrastructure and superstructure, so the system functions— thanks largely to American expertise and military protection. Otherwise, little is accomplished, despite self-serving newspaper headlines and television reports published in doublethink: "Saudi Geologists Discover Oil Reserves Near Mecca" (American scientists mapped the region in the 1930s); "Saudi Medical Researchers Find a Cure for Diabetes" (This claim was utterly false); "No US Military Presence in the Kingdom" (During break at the language institute, I traded jump stories with US Special Ops officers); "Thousands Cheer as King Fahd Returns to Riyadh (The streets were literally empty at 2:00 a.m., when the royal entourage passed beneath the fifteenth-story window of the tallest apartment building); and more of the same disinformation with every edition.

Political repression and religious fanaticism, which one cannot escape or ignore, permeate all aspects of society. Beginning with citywide prayer calls at dawn and continuing at intervals until dusk, when all shops, restaurants, and social activities cease for still another half-hour session in the scores of city mosques, the incessant fixation on Islam never ends. While I explained the fine points of the sonnet, a hand would shoot up. "Yes, Mohammed?"

"Sir, why aren't you a Muslim?"

"And why should I convert?"

"So we can all be brothers."

"What of Iran and Iraq, which are currently at war?"

"They are not good Muslims."

The Wahhabi sect of Sunni Islam defies belief. Women are subject to *purdah*, segregation, and seclusion. They cannot move about freely in the city—let alone go abroad—without an escort. The houses are divided by gender. After puberty women enjoy no contact with men outside trusted family members. Virgins are sold like precious goods for marriage, sight-unseen by either of the betrothed until the wedding night. The slightest violation of sexual mores means corporal punishment and/or execution as portrayed in the docudrama *Death of a Princess*. The *jelled* [punishment] is carried out, publically, in Deera Square, adjacent to the central mosque. Flogging, stoning, and beheading occur on Friday after prayers, the Muslim Sabbath spectacle. The crowd cheers in mob approval when a miscreant is decapitated, blood spurting like a scarlet geyser.

Riyadh with its Puritanical restrictions, Victorian dress code, Orwellian censorship, and various prohibitions concerning peaceful assembly, plus bans on alcohol, clandestine Christian prayer meetings, and fraternizing with the opposite sex (unless legally married) makes seventeenth-century Salem, Massachusetts resemble the Boston Combat Zone in the 1970s. Vulnerable Westerners, not surprisingly, snap.

On a regular basis, Saudi officials escort foreign experts to the airport in a virtually catatonic state. Other employees, through ignorance or small error in judgment, are arrested without charge and held in the local jail, sometimes indefinitely. Food is not provided by the prison administration, so relatives, friends or employers contribute dishes, which are inspected for contraband and distributed to the designated prisoners. Those without outside assistance do not starve, but sharing one's *kabsa* (the national dish made of rice and vegetables) may exact a terrible price. In Riyadh, nothing is free.

Yet despite informers, curfews, roadblocks, and constant surveillance, the human heart—infinite in cunning—has learned to deceive its vigilant keepers. Like incorrigible felons in maximum-security prisons, the Saudi citizens (aided and abetted by hordes of foreign workers) have created a black market in whisky, drugs, and pornography. These enterprises are expensive, given technical difficulties and risk, but no one is deprived of the usual vices, except (with some narrow exceptions) for sex. Owing to the human element, prostitution, though rare, could not be entirely eliminated, just greatly restricted. African Saudis without a husband or an extended family for protection and income sell a variety of nuts, piled on rugs, throughout the city. Typically, the vendors are obese and past their prime, many displaying tribal scars from below the hairline to the upper jaw. Their palms, decorated by intricate designs with vegetable dyes, are held in supplication to passersby.

Those lustful men who speak fluent Arabic utter the speakeasy verbal codes while ostensibly bargaining for a few ounces of Persian pistachios. With reckless courage, the desperate satyrs could make an arrangement: an uncomfortable coupling on a taxi backseat in the desert: a rendezvous (by all accounts) that would be nasty, brutish, and short. Rich citizens, of which there were many, enjoy a nearly foolproof option, but the illegal fornicators, married or single, did not share the wealth.

In exchange for oil, virtually all goods (including Australian camels) are imported. Dates, which grow in profusion atop palm trees along the road dividers, and bottled spring water from a nearby village are notable exceptions. Human female imports are accorded special treatment. Thus foreign women, deprived of their passports on arrival and assigned to apartments or villas to keep house and care for children, are literally up for grabs. Their employers routinely rape domestics, typically Thais or Filipinas. A student admitted to this practice, and when asked about unwanted pregnancy, replied nonchalantly, "I would then kill her." Chillingly, newspaper accounts occasionally report mysterious deaths, often glibly explained by the authorities and dutifully published by state controlled media: "Two Manila Nurse-maids Fall to their Death from a Balcony."

Homosexual practices, strictly illegal and in certain instances punishable by execution, flourish. Young boys, eager for satisfaction or pocket money, make blind house calls, reflecting the general attitude toward unbelievers: women are whores, and men are hustlers. Otherwise, the straight and single are left to their own solitary vices. Imaginative young men are thus deprived of the opportunity to report a fantasy encounter along the lines of, "I was hitchhiking, and this beautiful brunette, half drunk, picked me up. . ." Women cannot drive in Saudi.

As for potential co-ed trysts or flirtatious meetings during office hours, the university remains strictly segregated, with female instructors and their students relegated to another campus, under guard, located far from the main complex. Bars, nightclubs, and theatres are forbidden in Riyadh. Restaurants accommodate "families" (mixed couples), but no woman dines publically alone. The back of the bus, cordoned off by plywood to prevent eye contact, admits women from a rear entrance. These ladies never travel about the city by themselves. On one occasion during my three-year stay, the foreign faculty, male and female, met for an important meeting. We were instructed to sit across from one another at a long, wide, table.

The Saudi ethos is grounded in hypocrisy and intolerance. Contracts, insurance policies, and leases include strict provisions based on race, religion, and nationality. These codes are enshrined in the legal system, called "*sharia* law," which is based on sixth-century desert tribal codes. Alcohol is banned with zero exceptions. If caught drinking or in external/internal possession, the penalties are as certain as gravity.

Yet in every grocery store, grape juice, sugar, and yeast placed side-by-side line the shelves. As food or condiments, these items are in no way related, but those interested in making "sneaky pete" wine need not search the shop to find basic ingredients.

Bootleg whisky called *saddeeqi* [my friend] is readily available. Riyadh white lightning runs about 90 proof and tastes like battery acid. Few drink it straight more than once. Mixing it with fruit punch in limited quantities does not improve the flavor, but provides a guaranteed buzz. Members of the royal family, numbering in the thousands, can enter the Kingdom without undergoing a luggage search. Given a pass at the frontier, unscrupulous princes of the blood are bootleggers, making huge profits on every bottle of Johnny Walker, the whisky of choice. On holidays like Christmas (which is not officially observed in Riyadh) and New Year's Eve a fifth sells for $100 a bottle. The entrepreneur is sold out within hours.

Hard drugs are not unknown, but most Saudi addicts are content with amphetamines, which can be purchased, along with Valium and other barbiturates, over the counter without a prescription. Syringes are also dispensed at the local chemist, so strung-out Westerners, for the most part, can support their cocaine, morphine, or heroin habit—so long as they escape detection. Pot and hashish are also available.

Yet for every drug user, the Perfect System supports many more alcoholics. The common greeting upon visiting a friend recalls American Prohibition: "Want a drink?" During the occasional dry spells, when the police arrest bootleggers, desperate boozers buy and drink Aqua Velva, which can be toxic in large doses. A person sometimes pays to ride a public van, which serves as cheap citywide transportation, with wobbly passengers smelling like a barbershop.

Pornographic tapes, typically produced in Scandinavian countries, crowd the video shelf (in the all private male tearooms) next to tapes of soccer matches, Egyptian musicals, and *Lawrence of Arabia*. All tastes and persuasions are satisfied. After the host offers his guest a forbidden drink, he might say, "Want to watch a stag film?" Skin magazines, however, are not in evidence. During my stay, I never saw a copy of *Playboy*, *Stag*, or *Penthouse*—nor even pinup magazines, which have been readily sold in Western countries since the 1940s.

Each week, news-starved ex-patriots discovered innocuous publications like *Time* or *Newsweek* mutilated by censors. Offensive passages, articles, and entire pages had been cut out and deposited in the "memory hole." Certain events, ideas, and beliefs that occurred in the wider world did not exist in Saudi Arabia. Photos of women (including airline attendants, runway models, entertainers, and celebrities) were subject to a black felt-tip pen wielded by zealous guardians of public morals. Exposed flesh above the knee and the slightest hint of cleavage was blackened. According to rumor, young studs in the Panda supermarket would sometimes find themselves flashed by brazen nubile women, who would lurk in a food aisle and quickly pull aside their veils to reveal bronzed, hawk-like features and a dazzling smile. When I moved into my private apartment, a woman made obscene phone calls in Arabic, which I did not fully understand, though I got the idea. Male operators would eavesdrop, so one had to proceed with care.

My Saudi friends spoke of live sex shows and orgies for "invited guests only" at desert retreats. A reliable associate, who moonlighted as a mechanic, reported a swinger's party, but those events were rare, since news travels fast in a police state. No sensible person took the media seriously; consequently, rumors (utterly fantastic, but sometimes true) served to misinform the public. Urban myths, repeated as gospel, thrilled listeners. The tribal storyteller, despite modern architecture and air conditioning, flourished in Riyadh.

In the Magic Kingdom, the narrative ran from improbable (e.g., fifty Israeli commandos slipped over the southern border with Yemen and photographed the airport, which would be bombed on Yom Kippur) to the impossible (e.g., the king controls weather patterns). Though magic and superstition are *haram* [forbidden] by Islam, many educated, well-traveled, sophisticated Saudis believe absolutely in djinns (the root of the English word "genie"): shape-shifters which possessed sheep, goats, camels, but otherwise remained invisible.

According to local folklore, there was a variation on an Irish myth featuring banshees in which two teens on a shopping escapade slipped away from their minders and crashed a wedding party. They sneaked into the ladies' sector and beheld the female guests dancing, Western style, to the beat of drums and the eerie falsetto of flutes. One turned to the other with a terrified expression: "Wellah, look!" To their horror, the partygoers revealed their true being, each clopping around the wooden floor on goat and camel hooves. Screaming hysterically, the two teen girls ran into the street and flagged a taxi.

Once safe in the women's quarters, they told their mothers, half-sisters, aunts, and cousins the dreadful news. The house was in an uproar with weeping and wailing and the beating of breasts. Finally, the patriarch entered the kitchen to check the commotion. "What is the matter?" he shouted. "By Allah, show respect." The senior wife, stifling her sobs, told her master that the two girls, Fatima and Wellah, had witnessed a djinn assembly not far from that very spot. Doom was imminent. Mohammed paused, pondered the matter carefully, and with the authority of a desert sheik, pronounced his verdict. "It is written that there are more djinns in Riyadh than anywhere else in *dar es salaam* [the house of peace, the Arab world]— except for Oman."

However fantastic the stories, everyone understood that the state-run media was not concerned with reporting the truth—quite the opposite. I once announced to my shocked colleagues that the *Arab News* remained the most reliable paper in print. . .so long as one read it ironically.

Saudi TV served as a soporific for insomniacs. The two or three stations provided limited programming: endless footage of Mecca, *Sesame Street* in Arabic, and the unreliable news, typically announcing that the king (known officially as the "genius diplomat") was once again visiting his brother monarchs in the Emirates on state business. The contents of those high-level meetings and discussions remained top secret. However, the TV screens doubled as the technology required for video cassettes (some illegal, like *Death of a Princess* and

X-rated films); consequently, each household tearoom, for men only, featured a large-screen television set.

Given the kingdom's immense wealth and small population, the government truthfully boasted full employment. Illiterate *bedu*, already in their dotage, shuffled from office to office carrying thick folders and Dickensian ledgers of red tape. Self-important adolescents served as bank tellers and postal clerks. No one, except Palestinians, paid taxes of any description, and everyone received free medical/dental treatment from birth to burial. My three-bedroom apartment required five air conditioners, which ran continuously, since temperatures rarely drop below 103°F during the day. Yet my electricity bill ran about $9 per month. Middle-aged drivers spoke in wonder of 1950s gas prices when they pulled up to the pump. Basically, a populace of three million lived on the dole.

Moreover, students received a generous monthly stipend, with increments, as the scholar progressed from primary school to university. Male citizens, at eighteen, were eligible for a generous loan at zero interest to start a business. To my knowledge, no one felt obliged to repay the advance. The royal family (in their wisdom) commanded just 80% of the wealth, distributing largesse in various forms and amounts amongst the male citizenry—although the women benefited indirectly as well.

Unlike capitalist countries, Saudi Arabia actually offered any number of perks *gratis* and without the usual "small fee" as noted in the *West Side Story* lyric. Saudi salesmen, real estate agents, and shop owners listed prices in round numbers: Chevy pickup, used: 11,000SR; Villa, furnished, for rent: 100,000SR per annum; *shawarma* sandwich: 2SR. No string of 9s to mislead the buyer.

Yet the system was rigged and corrupt to the core. The governmental policy of outright bribery, along with the usual authoritarian restraining practices, kept the Perfect System running, after a fashion. Discretionary funds served an additional purpose: the opportunity for a brief respite from political/social repression and sublime boredom.

During my tenure, jet liners bound for Thailand, Manila, London, and New York filled to capacity on each international flight. In Bangkok, Thailand, where I lived and worked for six years, tourists from the Gulf soon changed the city's economy.

Thais, although friendly toward strangers and tolerant of most cultural differences, were opportunists. Taxi drivers, hotel owners, massage-parlor madams, food vendors, and tourist touts quickly took advantage of their wealthy customers. Prices soared and stabilized. By the early 1980s, a wild night in the Sukhumvit area—on Soi Cowboy or in Patpong—could still be had, but no longer for a few baht. Yet many visitors from the Middle East soon wore out their welcome by regularly staging drunken rages, wrecking hotel rooms, and forcibly sodomizing the *mahas* (young girls available for the price of a few meals plus a cheap dress or a pair of imported shoes), then fleeing the scene without paying the bill.

Signs appeared in bar windows: "Out of respect for Islam, no Arabs permitted inside." The tourist industry produced T-shirts with a cartoon of a pig in headgear bearing the legend "Sow-Dee"—the pun on the first word being obvious, and the second expression meaning "good" in Thai. Pork products were forbidden according to Islamic dietary restrictions, and the word "pig," when applied to people, connotated slovenly manners, dirty habits, and sexual depravity. That image and various ethnic restrictions targeting visitors from the peninsula hardly qualified as politically correct. However, many travelers and workers with some experience east of the Suez carried bitter memories of humiliation, injustice, exploitation, and abuse. As Gaugin noted, "Life being what it is, one seeks revenge." Or in the Vietnam military idiom, "My payback is a motherfucker!"

After the first semester, I had come to expect, but not welcome, spontaneous and unannounced absenteeism throughout the term. Professors were entitled to deduct points for student peccadilloes, but most of our young scholars were barely passing under the best of circumstances. In similar fashion, lifers often say (after breaking a prison regulation), "What are they going to do? I'm already in jail."

My teaching duties, after the first year, devolved to guiding the graduating seniors (less than half a dozen per annum) to the vacuous commencement ceremony, which might not have commenced, since I left
for summer break after the final spring term exam. No student,
administrator, associate, or colleague mentioned the short walk to
collect an unearned diploma.

By the 1980s, few Western students pursued a career in the humanities. The field peaked in the middle 1960s and rapidly declined there-
after. Young people turned their interest to medicine, the law,
business, and computer science: i.e., practical areas of expertise. In a
magazine article directed to job-seeking graduates, the author
observed, "Unless you have a prison record or a degree in the liberal
arts, assume you have something valuable to offer a prospective
employer during the interview." A Beckett play director changed the
final insult between the two tramps in *Waiting for Godot* from "critic"
to "humanist." By the end of the century, the sons and daughters of
Erasmus were a dying breed.

Nevertheless, the King Saud University board of directors understood
that prestigious American and European universities offered certifica-
tion in literature, so they hired four native-speaking professors as window dressing. With cost efficiency cast to the winds for the quixotic
enterprise, the Saudis spent a fortune annually to graduate a handful
of pidgin-speaking literature majors with few prospects. Moreover,
almost without exception, I directed non-Saudis in their studies:
Palestinians, Jordanians, North Africans, and Yeminis.

Our hosts met and exceeded physical needs. Teaching assignments
could not be measured realistically in "loads"; the administration
cancelled classes on a whim for such non-events as the king's successful operation or "rain days." However, our employers trounced
academic freedom and ignored professional expectations, such as
democratically run faculty meetings. On a monthly basis, policy
debate proceeded vigorously behind closed doors, followed by a
final pronouncement from the Chair, who took his orders from the
Dean, *in absentia*. I—along with my Western colleagues—contended

with irresponsible (though unfailingly personable) students, a flawed system, and incompetent, pretentious, Arabic-speaking faculty members posing as literature professors with little to profess. They clearly held to the biblical counsel: "There is too much reading of too many books, and much study is a weariness to the flesh."

My Middle East colleagues labored under no such concerns. After only a brief exchange at the first faculty meeting, the permanent members clearly demonstrated that they were virtually innocent of the Western canon, literary theory, and any critical methodology worth considering. "Hermeneutics" was not in their vocabulary. In the words of Harold Bloom, they preferred a *naïve* reading of texts for "boys and girls" like *The Red Pony, The Old Man and the Sea,* and *Lord of the Flies.* Regarding important canonical writers, their collective ignorance was appalling. Henry James, Virginia Woolf, William Faulkner, James Joyce, *et al.* remained for them unexplored territory. Cognate fields like psychology, anthropology, philosophy, semiotics, etc. never entered the discourse.

Abdul Kareem Mohammed al-Jerbazi, the unprepared, presumptuous Head of Department, glanced at the literary term "doppelgänger" and wondered aloud, "Who's this guy?" Abdul also hated *Moby Dick,* which he had probably never read and certainly did not understand or appreciate. "*Moby Dick!*" he once said contemptuously. "Too many times I see it on the list. Even the children's cartoon shows *Moby Dick.*" He paused and glared at me and my colleague, who had been hastily summoned to the head office for an emergency session on the American literature syllabus. "*Moby Dick,*" he muttered again. "I blame Hawari for this!"

In fact, Professor Hawari taught, by some definition, courses in English literature exclusively and most likely had not read the American masterpiece either. He did not serve on the curriculum committee for the logical reason that none existed. The Chair assigned courses, and the professors ordered the texts through a corrupt publisher's representative. The specific textbooks/editions might or might not arrive before classes began. However, my colleague and I were accustomed to the gratuitous *non sequitur*. Cynical ex-patriots referred to those lapses in sequential reasoning as "Saudi logic." After Abdu's outburst in which he assigned blame to an innocent party for the crisis, we grunted parting words, returned to our spacious carpet-lined office, and ordered tea, the national beverage.

Another *ex-officio* faculty member told his students that the single mention of the word "wheelbarrow" in the William Carlos Williams lyric on imagery called for a Marxist interpretation, which he did not explicate. When a student asked the same bogus scholar to interpret a poem by e.e. cummings, the instructor replied, "Read between the lines." No one could adequately explain how the academic frauds had almost to a man "earned" their degrees at prestigious American universities, including state-supported schools located in Arizona, Minnesota, and Indiana. The mystery provoked various explanations based solely on rumor and speculation. Certain theories, however, were persuasive.

One of my American-educated Lebanese friends (legitimate in this case) who taught at a different Riyadh college said that word had come down (unofficially) from the State Department: "More Saudi PhDs, to keep the light crude flowing smoothly." My officemate, an old Middle East hand, stated that translating dissertations into English from a foreign language like German was a common practice. I knew of a Saudi graduate student who invited his dissertation advisor to visit the Kingdom, all expenses paid, in order "to conduct research." One of my own scholars in full pursuit of the elusive BA invited me to visit his camera shop. I declined with thanks, since I understood the tactic: Upon admiring an expensive item such as a telephoto lens, he would present it as a gift, and to refuse an act of generosity would have been considered an insult. Likewise, an unwillingness to reciprocate in suitable fashion (with a respectable grade in that case) would also have been bad form.

Ahmed offered another suggestion: Why not make arrangements for a tutorial, held at the well-appointed family villa? He would provide transportation and refreshments for my convenience. Money, of course, was not so important, yet Ahmed was prepared to pay handsomely for my time and trouble. I again refused a transparent attempt to compromise my professional policy: grades were awarded by merit, not bought. Still, some of my esteemed colleagues agreed to the well-known deal, earnestly claiming no undue influence when calculating quality points at the end of the term. Counterituitively, an intellectual can rationalize *anything*: slavery, child prostitution, racism, nuclear war. . .

The students, like their high school teachers (typically, pretentious Egyptians with dubious credentials), were equally ignorant of Western culture and values. Though certainly not lacking in intelligence, by the time they matriculated at King Saud University it was already too late. With rare exceptions, Saudis viewed the world through the prism of Islam. A bright young man reported how Muslim scholars rewrote Freud's tripartite personality theory into ego (Mohammed), super-ego (Allah), and id (*ha-shatan* or Satan), thus making scientific doctrine a matter of religious belief. The students were hamstrung from the start.

A Fulbright scholar, Dr. Skitzers, asked me to fill in while he was away. He taught World Masterpieces and suggested I introduce his charges to Dostoyevsky's *The Idiot*. I spent part of the hour explaining that the term "idiot" in that context did not mean a low intelligence quotient, but rather innocence. Specifically, Prince Myshkin was a virgin. The students seemed content with that clarification. After class, however, a youngster named "Mohammed" approached my desk, the picture of consternation. "Sir," he began haltingly, "thank you for the lecture. I take notes. But sir, I never had sex. I swear to the God I never had sex. . . Am I an idiot?"

Arabs were taught to bargain from the time they learned to speak, and that ingrained habit remained integral to their worldview. A colleague announced a quiz. "Does spelling count, sir?" a student enquired. "Indeed," my friend replied. "Can I bring a dictionary?" the boy wanted to know. "Absolutely not," his professor replied. "Well, can I bring a small dictionary?"

The administration, on the other hand, kept a sharp and jaundiced eye on teaching practices. From long, bitter experience, they had learned that Christian foreigners, presumed devout but sadly mistaken in choosing the Bible over the Koran, might deliberately or even unconsciously proselytize under cover of sharing knowledge and wisdom. In one notable instance, a Milton scholar lost his job for interpreting *Paradise Lost* as a primarily Christian poem.

Our students typically gave Western emphasis on charity, sympathy, and forgiveness short shrift. During a private discussion over *shai*, I mildly objected to punishment by the sword, lethal or otherwise. "But you have to remember the criminal's bad crime," my student protested. "I don't care what he might have done," I said. "You don't carve up a human being like a roast." He hesitated for a moment and said with finality, "Well, it will teach him a good lesson."

I soon concluded that political/social repression foregrounded the worst in people, affecting negatively both those who enforced draconian laws as well as the victims who suffered, at least psychologically, on a daily basis.

Typically, paper shufflers, security officers, motorists, and even shop owners were obnoxious, verbally aggressive, and gratuitously rude to unbelievers or non-Saudis. On the other hand, foreign workers, numbering in the tens of thousands, were surly and resentful, eagerly inventing, accepting, and repeating outrageous conspiracy theories concerning their hosts. When a plane cleared Saudi airspace, Westerners aboard broke into spontaneous applause, to the undoubted humiliation of the Gulf passengers. Soon after landing at the London airport, tough British oil riggers, on a bet, occasionally decked a Saudi citizen. Flush with petro-quid, the gang gladly paid the fine (assuming the "bobbies" bothered to make an arrest) for simple assault.

Within two years I had learned rudimentary Arabic, avoided social taboos, practiced civil behavior by local standards, and re-evaluated my own cultural values and beliefs. Consequently, study, travel, research, and friendship paid off in both *riyals* and personal benefits. I reaped considerable rewards, including a first-class round trip to Jordan, where I attended a conference and tour of Petra, an invitation to the King's Jubilee ceremony at the palace on the once-forbidden royal boulevard, an opportunity to review scholarly essays submitted to the house organ at $150 an article, and general acceptance, though necessarily limited, by my Arabic-speaking colleagues and students.

Yet I became increasingly aware that a false sense of security meant something quite different: the very real possibility of arbitrary arrest, deportation, and physical/mental breakdown. Each morning I awoke to conversations in Arabic outside my bedroom window. The faithful rose at dawn to attend prayers; afterward, men lingered about the neighborhood, smoking and talking, until the teashops opened for morning trade. The human alarm clock triggered two strong emotions: anxiety and rage. With no respite after several weeks, I concluded it was time to pack my bags, get my hat, flee the scene, split, book, take French leave. . .

Specifically, I decided to resign the self-renewing contract and head for Thammasat University in Bangkok, Thailand, which I had visited during the *hajj* break in 1982. On impulse, I sat for an unofficial interview followed by a letter of application. In due time, the Chair of Liberal Arts made me an offer, which in view of the miniscule salary—especially when compared to my Saudi pay packet—was easy to refuse. But I kept my options open, hedged my bets.

To further complicate matters, Dr. Abdul invited me to his office for a private discussion. He had spoken with the Dean about raising my already princely stipend—on the condition I agree to teach at King Saud for at least two more years. I seriously considered the tempting offer, since upon completing and surviving five punishing rounds, a King Saud employee was entitled to a munificent bonus, which came to twice the usual amount. Thus I faced the classic dilemma: easy money with little responsibility versus well-being and self-respect.

Given the American economy and my investment portfolio, already fat, I calculated that after even two more years in harness, I would almost certainly be financially set for life. I also understood clearly that my physical condition and mental stability were at risk. A stroke, heart attack, adult onset of diabetes, and various other middle-age health crises loomed on the near horizon. In fact, I was already and for the first time not only obese, but developing symptoms. Over summer break in London, a Harley Street doctor had diagnosed, after only one year in the Magic Kingdom, hypertension and a high cholesterol count.

Even more importantly, I sensed—like T.S. Eliot, Ernest Hemingway, F. Scott Fitzgerald, and John Berryman, among other writers I admired—an incipient nervous breakdown. In stressful Saudi, my free and easy demeanor, which set everybody at ease, had soon vanished. My behavior changed for the worse: suspicious, judgmental, guarded, and hypersensitive. I no longer accepted well-meant comments at face value; I brooded on real or imagined slights and lost sleep; I ate chocolate-caramel candy bars and drank a dozen or more sugar-saturated Pepsis per day, in addition to endless glasses of equally over-sweet tea. Clearly, still in my prime, I was headed for end credits.

I gave the decision—to stay or to leave—serious thought. Existential choice is over-determined; no one takes the leap for a single reason. Most depend, however, on a basic, personally reliable authority, like religion or philosophy. When facing a crisis, I have always consulted literature for life's lessons, often by negative example. The tragic flaw destroyed noble princes like Oedipus and Agamemnon. Macbeth should have been content with his title earned in battle, but he wanted more and suffered the inevitable fall. Captain Ahab was obsessed with revenge, and Roskolnikov considered himself superior, above moral law. Thanks to those and numerous other models of bad judgment demonstrated by literary characters, I had learned better.

I recalled the final scene in Marlowe's *Dr. Faustus*, who fully realized his mortal mistake, but too late. Faust quoted Ovid as the witching hour drew near: "O, run slowly, slowly, horses of the night." Desperate, he prayed for a reprieve, but the Devil's contract, signed in blood, had to be redeemed—and to the letter. At the stroke of midnight, the demons were at hand: no going back.

I do not believe in an immortal soul, but I put a great deal of faith in my *mind*. The night before the resignation deadline, with my eighteen-month bonus plus various stipends in the balance, I called *Arjan Dittya*, getting her out of bed, to accept the offer at Thammasat. Next term, I would fly to Bangkok after the monsoon season—no signed contract, but essentially a done deal.

The next day I wrote a short letter to Dr. Jerbazi: my sojourn in the Magic Kingdom had run its course. Abdu, who had expected me to remain on board through the decade, did not understand my decision to leave, forever, the Perfect System. He asked me to reconsider my foolish choice; after all, he implied, how many middle-class Americans strike it rich well before turning fifty? I listened, replied *"ma'salaama,"* and booked my flight.

I lived in Thailand for six years, never leaving the country, and thoroughly enjoyed the tropical climate, the food, my classes, and overall, the people in The Land of Smiles. As for the Perfect System and its offer of treasure, I never looked back.

II.

Teaching the Good, the True, and the Beautiful

How wondrous this, how mysterious!
I hew wood, I draw water.—Zen poem

In September 1983, I arrived in Krung Thep (better known as Bangkok) during an extended rainy season. The entire downtown area flooded. Teenage boys cast nets in the stream flowing down Sukhumvit (the city's Broadway) and tossed the catch into large white buckets. Fishing was excellent, as the well-stocked, private ponds overflowed, and the whoppers swam downstream, temporarily free at last. Shop owners lost their bottom shelf of goods to water damage. Business, for the most part, remained suspended for weeks. The English-language newspaper featured daily editorials. Millions of *baht* for Dutch pumps had disappeared, and no one could account for the missing money, a perennial problem. Who was to blame that year? Finally, a government underling defended the embattled Minister of the Interior: "Mr. Banomyong can't stop the rain."

Having resigned my post at King Saud University in April and conducted a phone interview with the Chair of the Literature Department in Bangkok, I was hired to teach at Thammasat University on the swollen Chao Phraya River. When the muddy waters breached the banks, the administration cancelled classes. Meanwhile, with the help of a hotel clerk, I found permanent lodging a short cab ride from the university. The next day I found myself high and dry in The President House, where I rented apartment #1 for the following six years.

True, I had faced an unexpected development, but no reason to panic. A common Thai expression nicely covered the situation: *mai pen rai* or "never mind," which was understood literally. One does not necessarily require wealth, influence, exceptional intelligence, language skills, or similar advantages to cope psychologically in exotic cultures, but one must "go with the flow." I came to understand that the East, despite the handy phrase, couldn't be described as "mysterious." But the Orient also shared few parallels with Hackensack, New Jersey.

The furnished four-room flat featured a modest sitting room, small kitchen, smaller bathroom/shower, and one air conditioner, which I rarely used, preferring a fan. The accommodation included maid and laundry service, both dependable. I am not known for fastidious house cleaning or neat apparel. Friends and family members on the first visit exclaimed, "*You* live here?" The polished rosewood floors glowed; the dishes sparkled on the drain board; my clothes, clean and pressed, hung in the closet; the freshly made bed could have passed military inspection.

Ped ("Duck"), my housekeeper, lined Pepsi bottles like soldiers on drill in the fridge and carefully arranged seafood, fruit, and vegetables on the shelves. My discarded texts and foul papers appeared in perfect order in the large, bamboo bookcase. A convenient pool beckoned a few steps from the front door. Well placed, since the temperature/humidity held steady in the nineties, requiring several dips per day. No winter temperatures in Bangkok, which stayed hot year-round. As in the *Porgy and Bess* lyric, "The livin' is easy"—for "rich" *farang* [foreigners] like myself and elite Thai families at least. The remaining population had to hustle, beg, borrow, or steal to survive.

Two distinct social classes have evolved in Thailand: exceptionally wealthy and dirt-poor. Laborers earned about three dollars a day. Officials lived well, but not on government salaries. Dostoyevsky's Svidrigailov confessed, "I never gamble at cards. I cheat." In similar fashion, successful Thais were on the fiddle. Random examples: massage parlors (brothels) were located throughout the city, and juke joints featured pole dancers who would spend the night with anyone willing to pay the "bar fine" plus her fee, which was negotiable. Prostitution was illegal. Vendors, which thrived at all hours throughout the city, operated without a license. Police demanded bribes to supplement a meager income.

It got worse. Smuggling infractions, traffic violations, and misdemeanors could be resolved by a bottle of whisky or a few *baht*. Security officers occasionally set up a roadblock and required money to pass. Thailand formed part of the Golden Triangle, and drugs abounded. Users were generally ignored, though dealing heroin (outside the Thai mafia, which operated with impunity) was a capital offense. Thai sticks (potent marijuana) went for $1 a pop. Middlemen sold artifacts pilfered from ruins, and poachers captured/killed rare animals for sale or export. Cobra and tiger blood were held to increase longevity and potency, and the former aphrodisiac was available at the entrance of Lumpini Park, while the latter panacea, which was expensive, had to be obtained from the *demimonde*. All manner of potions made from endangered animal products were sold in Chinatown pharmacies. Curio shops stocked snake-skin belts, monkey skulls, crocodile handbags/briefcases, and similar items.

In brief, the entire system was corrupt. Yet those without means and power did not profit from illegal enterprises. If caught, they simply paid the price: years of imprisonment for comparatively minor offenses and execution for capital crimes. Families at the top were not only rich but also highly influential, and favors were for sale. A person in distress might have consulted a fixer, the "Big Noodle," for assistance. Thus, the sole criterion for satisfactory results remained universal: money. Although I could presumably afford a player's fee, I avoided lucrative temptations on offer such as business partnerships, real estate investments, drug deals, and similar enterprises. I knew of, but never met, the Big Noodle.

In the event, I politely refused a number of offers "guaranteed" to pay dividends for life, while a number of friends and acquaintances lived to regret decisions informed by greed. An American or European foreign expert living in an upscale apartment complex, taking cabs (as opposed to overcrowded buses) for transportation, eating occasionally at the Hotel Orient, traveling often, supporting women, and so on must be wealthy—providing no end to mutually beneficial opportunities. Thais on the make welcomed foreign sponsors.

By Western standards, no one would have pronounced me rich. Given the Thai economy, however, I lived comfortably on a meager university salary. I soon learned to bargain in Thai and avoid extravagant habits such as frequent trips to the seaside resorts, off-shore islands, and popular overseas junkets to Singapore, Malaysia, and the Philippines. I joined the Clark Hatch Fitness Center, which charged a monthly fee, to keep in shape, and frequented upscale restaurants as opposed to vendors and family-owned chop suey joints on occasion, but otherwise managed on a frugal budget.

My teaching responsibilities demanded little time (except for grading essays) or effort. When friends asked about the course load and teaching standards, I had a ready answer: "Well, teaching here is like a highly subsidized vacation; sometimes, I have to *de*-prepare for my classes." During my stay, I did not serve on committees or attend faculty meetings. Conferences were virtually unknown, though I read papers on psychoanalytic criticism at the behest of my colleagues, who invited several professors from nearby Chulalongkorn (seriously called "the Harvard of the Far East") for the presentations.

The society was structured according to a strict hierarchy, with the top tier divided (unevenly) among three divisions: royalty, religious authorities, and *arjans*, i.e., university professors. As an American middle-aged male employed at the second-largest university, I enjoyed an elevated social status. I refused, however, to treat/address anyone as an inferior, whose distinction was built into the language. I simply avoided the pronouns denoting social rank and spoke to everyone as an equal.

Since spoken Thai bore no resemblance to Greek and Latin roots, the usual points of reference (Germanic/ Romance languages) for native English speakers were not available. Thus, upon arrival, basic communication presented a problem outside the President House compound. With few exceptions, no one on *Khlong* [canal] *Prapa*, which ran alongside my *soi* [lane], spoke English. Having visited Sin City (Bangkok's well-earned byname) on break from Saudi the year before, I knew the drill. The hookers spoke a smattering of English, along with German and Arabic, required for trade. Consequently, I hailed a cab for Hotel Nana, which was located on a midtown street that ran slightly downhill. After paying the driver, I hoisted my trousers to negotiate soggy steps to the entrance, which featured a wooden barrier to deflect water from the coffee shop.

Inside, the booths were crowded with young girls, whom I designated "talented amateurs." Thus, the women (coincidentally, "farmers' daughters" from upcountry) provided services ranging from tour guide and interpreter to language instructor and childcare. Moreover, the girls slept with their customers, not for a fixed fee, but free love was unknown; the accommodating ladies expected/demanded gratuities (clothes/money in addition to meals, transportation, room rental) for their time and expertise. One could arrange for a more permanent partner at a reasonable sum. Along with the above specialties, working-class Thais were unfailingly excellent cooks and housekeepers, so a foreign expert might have hired a "rent-a-wife," potentially confirmed at the embassy.

I approached the nearest booth and said, "All right, girls, who likes to play sixty-nine?" Laughing and giggling like school kids, they chanted "siky-nine, siky-nine," since the "x" phoneme (as the interchangeable "l"/"r" and the "sh" diphthong is pronounced "ch") was difficult for a native speaker. Once seated, I felt a slim arm press my shoulder, and the girl next to me whispered, "I don't know, but I try, okay? Not too much for money," she added slyly. Fortuitously, the waiter appeared, and I ordered my hopeful companion a Coke. I didn't want her to lose face, since I had been kidding. I also understood that oral sex was not generally practiced among Thais—though notable exceptions occurred. A friend asked about his short-time girlfriend's reluctance to indulge his fellatio request, and she answered, "Buddha no suck!" On the other hand, young women on the game might have added an appendix to the *Kama Sutra* before turning twenty-one.

The standard greetings followed a predictable pattern of questions: "Where you come from?"; "You want girlfriend?"; and "We go chopping?" After a brief exchange, I invited an engaging young lady to the counter, where she provided the Thai equivalent to the list of useful words/phrases that included food, the number system to one hundred, place names, and useful nouns/verbs, along with greetings, basic negotiations, refusals, and other common expressions. Within a half hour, I felt confident enough to function without simply pointing and playing charades. My translator requested *seeseep* [40] *baht* for the tutorial, and I gave her fifty, enough for a snack and a ride in a three-wheeled vehicle called a *"tuk tuk,"* since the ladies were always on the move.

Compared to English, which is not highly inflected but distributed, spoken Thai is a pidgin language. For example, *"bai nai?"* means literally "go where?" Grammatical features like mood, tense, gerunds, participles, etc. do not exist. Uninflected markers are sometimes required, but context and situation carry meaning as well. Ruefully, I remembered endless Latin noun declensions and verb conjugations, the seven cases, and more complicated grammatical paradigms that had earned me a failing grade in Exploratory Languages as a junior-high-school student. To speak basic Thai, however, the learner must hear and use tones properly, which are semantically bound. A minor error results in total loss of communication. On several occasions, *tuk tuk* drivers looked baffled and roared off before I had completed a sentence. One or more false tones had produced nonsense diction, and the driver "fled the scene"—the Thai response to an awkward, embarrassing, confrontational incident.

Uneducated Thai English speakers made themselves understood, but often bemused the interlocutor. In *Culture Shock Thailand*, Robert Cooper related the following promise: "I'll do it today. And if I don't do it today, I'll do it three day." A friend asked his wife why, in the sex capital of the world, so many male homosexuals ignored endless opportunities to enjoy women. "Now, very popular," she explained. "Well, what's the matter, don't they like to fuck?" he asked. "They like to suck," she replied. Another friend invited a girl from the massage parlor to his hotel room and told her that he intended a night of intense lovemaking. "I not worried about it," she declared.

My command of the language after six years remained minimal. Yet no one commented on my lack after asking, *"Poot Thai, dai mai* [Do you speak Thai]?" when I answered, *"Nit noy"* or *"a little."* On leaving the country, however, the minor official who had issued the required exit visa was outraged when, after she announced we would conduct the conversation in Thai, I said, "My vocabulary is not good enough." Playing the schoolmarm, the lady dressed me down for my deficiency: "After all these years and never left the country!" I had failed to heed the advice of an old Asian hand: "Get yourself a sleeping dictionary. You'll be speaking fluent Thai in just a few months." On my first trip to Bangkok in 1981, I had tried that method. During a passionate embrace with my intrepid guide and translator, she cried, "Cleep! Cleep! I coming now," but I passed on an opportunity to learn an important phrase. But of course my advisor had meant a long-term arrangement, not a one-night stand.

As for language acquisition Bangkok-style, I had demurred for several reasons. A serious conversation with a long-time partner with no formal education remained unlikely. I prefer an engaging personality to Hollywood pulchritude. Foreigners, especially Americans who prized independence, failed to understand parental obligations in Thai culture. Moreover, older siblings could make unreasonable demands. Thais tended to take advantage, and a rich *farang* was a prime target, a fat lamb to be fleeced. As a case in point, my Los Angeles friend Don Freeland married his Bangkok girlfriend and set up housekeeping. To escape pollution and other big-city hazards, he bought a farm near Chiang Mai, the former capital, which was located north of Bangkok. He planned to build. A Thai national, however, by law was required to sign legal documents, so his wife technically owned the real estate. Her mother promptly demanded the title in order to operate a duck farm. When my friend visited his property, he found his mother-in-law well ensconced in her newly acquired place of business. Stunned foreigners, ignorant of contract law, familial obligations and commonplace consequences, regularly reported similar surprises in the English-language newspaper.

Then in my forties, I had acquired a measure of good judgment, thus avoiding traps baited and set for unwary *farang*. Attractive young women offered themselves like stage-door groupies crowding a rock star. By the early 1980s, however, an HIV infection meant certain death, and the available ladies were by and large oblivious to the dangers of unprotected sex. A government spokesman declared that Thais were blessed with a special gene protecting them from STDs, and only foreigners carried the deadly virus. In "never mind" fashion, many prostitutes accepted the deadly lie and contrived their own self-serving response. As a case in point, a Western reporter interviewed a sex worker who declared, "If a customer has a thin behind, I make him take a good chower first." Another said, "No other job to support my children. Hope I don't get sick." Thus, in the midst of sexual plenty, I basically starved.

However, I made good use of my time by reading, preparing articles for publication, and strolling the nearby canal most evenings to bat-watch. Despite lax standards at the university, I enjoyed teaching my students, who were mostly women. Thammasat did not admit married scholars, so the educated ladies were presumed virgins. And upper class parents were vigilant. The girls typically lived with an extended family in guarded compounds, and a chauffer drove his charges to and from school. Parents and adult relatives evaluated suitors like a connoisseur tasted rare wine. A parental veto was absolute, rarely contested by the hopeful fiancé. No one eloped in Thai society. An engagement might last several years, and most brides consummated the marriage in the nuptial chamber. Regarding sexual behavior, Bangkok was a culture of extremes. A young hustler observed, "Everyone fuck at sixteen. No fuck, no good." Her wealthy, educated sisters, whom I taught and knew from friendly conversation for years, rarely alluded to copulation and never in crude terms. My female students, who wore modest uniforms, did not address delicate topics in class or essays.

In America and abroad, I corrected student papers for decades and, although some were well written and expressed original ideas, few caught my attention intellectually. Those professors who humbly thank their students in book acknowledgements for teaching them about their own subjects are either fudging or incompetent. Thai insights, however, often proved delightful, as the following exam passages illustrate:

1. "The high class persons will meet at The Rainbow to dine, dance and talk happily. The rich like to feed horses."

2. "Gulliver eats very much like a greedy."

3. "In this story the villain is always after the heroin.

4. "Therefore, we must care, love, kind to everyone including poor people because they are human not subject. If we start to have soft, sensitive feeling more, it's not too late at all, when that day comes, we will live peacefully in Utopia land."

5. "When I finish reading Silas Marner, I relief since the happy ending I wish come true. I love this way of writing which is comedy of manners because happiness can be found and life is hopeful."

6. "But it is the fact that nothing is steadily. Nowadays the material world is rapidly progressive while human's soul is so evil. Man tries to make as much money as he can without caring for the other poor. Bartleby tries to find the best way for his life. (Of course that way is not making money.) But he can't find it, so one way to solve his problem is suicide."

Outside the classroom, butchered English and unintended double entendres appeared on T-shirts and advertisements, as a cruise brochure promised: "Very friendly and well-trained hostess under splendid captain."

A college senior out of uniform (and surely innocent of the risqué meaning) sported a T-shirt featuring an inebriated cat curled in a champagne glass, reading, "Happiness is a tight pussy." Another young woman most likely did not understand the legend, "I've been out of work for so long I can't even get a blow job!" emblazoned on her shirt.

Fortuitously, a common nickname, "*Nook*," means "bird." Most girls having no understanding of the English slang "nooky." For a prime example of unintended irony, a misprint substituted "c" for "d" on police cadet T-shirts that read "Every Man Has Price."

Understandably, my students were not well versed in Western culture. Few recognized or understood allusions, well-worn quotes/idiomatic expressions, place names, historical figures, or commonplace philo-sophical/psychological terms known to every American schoolboy. Generally, the symbolic/figurative levels of interpretation escaped their comprehension and passed unnoticed. I spent entire class peri-ods explaining context and plot/character devices in unchallenging poems, novels and essays. Yet graduating seniors requested cutting-edge seminar topics (gleaned from lectures/reading) for the open course during final semester. Consequently, during my tenure I taught specialized seminars in feminist literature, African American studies, and history of Western ideas with predictably mediocre results.

During office hours, I casually mentioned my abiding interest in the postmodern novel and turned to the topic at hand. To my surprise, the honors committee requested that difficult specialty for the elect semi-nar. Delighted with an opportunity to examine favorite postmodern novels, I listed *Pale Fire*, *Speedboat*, *Slaughterhouse Five*, and *Who Censored Roger Rabbit?* on the syllabus, expecting a solipsistic experience—like lecturing to an empty room. For two weeks I explained relevant features such as fabula/syuzhet, mixed genres, ontological character sta-tus, enthymeme, and paralogy, supplemented by critical methodologies borrowed from philosophy, psychology, linguistics, and other cognate subjects. My charges took notes but rarely raised a hand. Unexpectedly, those who stayed the course passed handily, and several students earned legitimate As and Bs. So much for predictions! I drew the tentative conclusion that Thais might actually think that way—confirming Nietzsche's concept of perspectivism in a manner no Western student of philosophy could anticipate.

Although teaching proved enjoyable, my years in Thailand could not be described as productive—at least by American academic standards. My two or three publications passed unnoticed, since brandishing accomplishments in the usual fashion was not appreciated by the administration; specifically, my Chair, who had long since hung up her scholarly gloves, would have lost face. Meanwhile, I read with a measure of depth favorite genres such as biography, the twentieth-century novel, and literary theory.

Lulled by the gentle rhythm of teaching, reading, training, and entertaining guests, the years passed quickly, until one day I experienced a moment of clarity: growing old in Thailand! A few weeks later, I politely declined the *pro forma* two-year contract, not expecting more than an expression of regret from the Chair, my colleagues, students, and the various associates who comprised modest arrangements with functionaries, cab drivers, bank officers/clerks, etc. Owing to my responsible and civil behavior, however, the Thais had not only appreciated my role as a professor and customer, but had accepted me as an honorary "family" member—not literally, of course, but as a distant, endearing relative worthy of special consideration. I soon realized my predicament: "*Ajarn*, why you leave us so soon!" Clearly, most everyone who knew me beyond a polite greeting expected me to remain happily ensconced in the Land of Smiles. After all, unlike my native-speaking counterparts and American/European assistants, I had remained in country.

I'm not fond of dissembling, but no decent person insults his hosts. I firmly decided to leave for several reasons, including the fact that I had accepted the "Thai way" all too well. The time factor had lost its precision, and the years were melting into an unfocused, sliding present: one day, one season, and—shockingly—one year dissolving into the next. Most Thais were amenable to that mode, but I was approaching fifty and did not want to die far from home. Clearly, time to flee the scene. After all, I reasoned, much to see, experience, and suffer yet; the Thai gig had been played out after six years.

As a colleague in Riyadh had warned, "Don't stay in the East for too long, or you'll lose the cutting edge." Compared to most Americans building a career, I was not well honed from the start, and Thailand positively rewarded a phlegmatic temperament. At Thammasat University, personal goals, deadlines, and high expectations did not obtain. To satisfy everyone concerned, a foreign expert must simply fulfill professional responsibilities, avoid political inference, and shun cultural taboos like *lèse majesté*, dating students, and disrespecting shrines.

Upon reflection, I provided an acceptable explanation for early departure: I hadn't seen my elderly father in many years. Surely no Thai could object. My Chair then suggested I take an unpaid leave of absence and return the following semester. I replied with the ambiguous, "We'll see." Shortly before departure and over my objections, favorite students arranged a party, and the college Dean, who had signed my departure documents, gave me an expensive handmade wallet and the promise of another contract: "Just let us know." After clearing the exit visa formalities, I bought a one-way ticket to New York, packed my luggage, invited close friends to a final seafood dinner, and boarded a jet for the Big Apple.

After arriving in the States, I remained active but unemployed at my brother's house. Although I enjoyed several months of vacation with no schedule or pressing concerns, I suffered reverse culture shock compounded by mild disorientation until, unexpectedly, a former Saudi colleague, then Assistant Director of a writing program, offered me a job. Fall term I accepted a post at a no-nonsense American university, which operated with military precision via computers. Adept at the infernal machines, the Department Head tracked both students and faculty members like NASA observing UFOs to the nanosecond.

My New Jersey colleagues were widely read, friendly, and personable, but intensely career driven, rendering social concerns secondary. During a typical conversation, my interlocutor might exclaim, "Cliff, I'd like to talk more about your overseas adventures, which are fascinating, but I have an appointment this afternoon at Princeton. Keep in touch." Thus, although living only fifty miles from the town where I was born, I failed to make a single, lasting friend.

Second semester I applied to Bilkent University, which offered me a contract in millions of Turkish *lira* (though considerably less in USD) and free lodging on campus. Soon after arrival, I found that the Turks were comparatively well organized and goal oriented, but I adjusted easily. When slippage inevitably occurred, I murmured a Bangkok idiom: *"Mai pen rai."*

III.

Profiles: Sweating It Out in Krung Thep

My strength is as the strength of ten, because my heart
is pure.—Sir Galahad

I am comfortable in the company of eccentrics, winos, counter-culture
individualists, and denizens of the tenderloin regardless of nationality, race, religion, or ethnic identity. Like Will Rogers, I rarely meet a
man or woman I don't like. It's the long haul at close quarters that
tests my patience and tolerance for abrasive traits. Barring neo-Nazis
and those with a similar mindset, everyone gets a fair hearing, at least
during the honeymoon period.

But the Bangkok gym did not fit the above low-rent criteria. The
upscale Hilton, within walking distance of the British Embassy,
fronted Wireless Road with a quiet *soi* bordered by a deep *khlong* running a hundred yards from the rear entrance. The area between the
hotel and the lane featured a large outdoor pool and a bosky pathway
populated by exotic frogs clinging like multicolored clay lumps on the
broad leaves and camouflaged lizards that skittered along the flag-
stones leading to the tennis courts, juice bar, massage salon, and
weight room. A handball court, occasionally commandeered for practice matches by karate and *Muay Thai* players, flanked the gym. In the
fitness center class, hierarchies, which were strictly observed throughout Thailand's complex social structure, dissolved; those with titles,
degrees, and pedigree left their prejudices, bigotry, superior attitudes,
and xenophobic convictions at the door.

Thailand is a monarchy. King Adulyadej, whose influence is unchal-
lenged, only intervenes in political affairs during times of crisis, since
Thai officials are fond of bloodless (and sometime bloody) coups.

Parliament, which is largely comprised of high-ranking military officers, conducts ordinary legal and bureaucratic affairs amidst bickering, squabbling, and name-calling. A minister is not above referring to a political rival as a "hooligan" or accusing an official of practicing witchcraft. During one political demonstration held near my apartment complex, I saw two or three insurgents hanging from street lamps as I glanced from a taxicab. The driver, whom I knew well, made no comment, looking straight ahead at oncoming traffic.

The crown prince, who regularly sires illegitimate children with his minor wife, is corrupt. Only the king by popular belief is exempt from bribery, nepotism, kickbacks, extortion, and outright theft. Wealthy families hire scholars to take entrance exams at the top universities. Thai faculty members often translate scholarship into their own language, which is written in a distinct dialect with Sanskrit letters few people, including most Thais, can read beyond signs, menus, newspapers, and the like. The bogus articles and books are submitted for publication and promotion. A suitable bribe ensures matriculation at one of the many diploma mills that appears like mushrooms throughout the capital.

Moreover, the pretense of a democratic state is risible, and the active discrimination toward citizens of Chinese background resembles the Jim Crow laws of post-Civil War America. Sino immigrants are assigned a "Thai" surname for instant identification. For example, one of the important Thai-Chinese banking families is saddled with "Big Stinking Canal" on their required identification cards and passports. Yet Thai Chinese tend to thrive in all segments save the military, which restricts officer rank to indigenous citizens.

By contrast, the fitness center, owned by an American body builder from the Midwest, welcomed all comers without exclusion or discrimination; Buddhists, Hindus, Christians, and Muslims mingled without distrust or dislike. American/European members spotted Thai, Malaysian, Indian, and Laotian weightlifters, and in return, our Asian friends in training demonstrated their penchant for hospitality and polite manners. The democratic atmosphere prevailed. Thus, old and young, fit and obese, man and woman all treated one another in a civil, cooperative manner with almost never a testy exchange or sarcastic comment. I once found a politely worded note taped to my locker stating that my sweat-soaked, abominable workout gloves had been confiscated and disposed of. "No offense!"

I first met John Hull, the British-born manager, at a twenty-kilometer run organized by the military to celebrate the liberation from communist insurgents, who during the Vietnam War had established an illegal enclave in a mountainous region near the northern border. The community had been self-sufficient, complete with schools, a hospital, and a rudimentary jail for miscreants.

After the exhaustive run, further challenged by a steep mountain trail, all participants enjoyed a barbecue, Western style. A British Embassy official introduced me to the decorated general who had planned and participated in the three-day campaign to reclaim the area. I asked him about particulars, and he said his military counterpart, trained in Russia, had escaped capture and summary execution. Intelligence officers had arrested Comrade Tanwat in Bangkok within days. "And the consequences?" I asked. "Oh, he's on our side now," the general replied, smiling. Thais, I learned, are not only tolerant but also forgiving.

After the picnic, I commented on the obvious fact that John worked out regularly. "Right," he replied in a Midlands accent. "I manage a fitness center behind the Bangkok Hilton. Anyone can join for a fortnight to try out the facilities for three quid. After that, a monthly fee." About a week later, I made an appointment for my evaluation. The physical exam was administered by a female staff member whose English was restricted to Tarzan phrases. "You try here," as I stepped on the scales or "Accuse me" as she looped a tape measure around my bulging middle. Using calipers on the thigh, chest, back, and love handles, she declared my body-fat ratio as 22%, while 10% was closer to ideal. The trainer then dropped a bamboo key holder and motioned for me to pick it up, knees locked. My joints creaked, and I suffered a severe dizzy spell as the blood rushed to my head. The trainer grinned in a passive-aggressive manner: "Not so good." Finally, I endured the horizontal weight test, a ten-pound bar bell in each hand, for less than five seconds, my arms shaking like palsy from the start.

John observed the procedure from a distance, bulging forearms across his hirsute chest, wide as an oven. He approached, notepad in hand, for the questionnaire portion of the test. "What do you eat for breakfast?" he asked. "I haven't had a standard morning meal more than a dozen times since about 1956," I replied. Frowning, he recorded my answer and said, "That's your first mistake. How many soft drinks per day?" I cleared my throat. "Well, I usually have about a half dozen Pepsis in warm weather." John groaned. "Any exercise preferences?" he asked, hopefully. "Well, as you know, I like to run. I was a lifeguard, and, with the outside pool available, I can always swim a few laps." John made a note. "You have the buoyancy for it," he said quietly. And so the examination proceeded.

Familiar with grading policies, I calculated a C- with no quality points for my less-than-stellar evaluation. I avoided outright failure by reporting truthfully that I ran along *Khlong Prapa* at a good clip for about an hour each morning. John, unimpressed, confirmed my suspicions. "Listen, mate, you should start a training program right away. No slacking off, now. If you push on daily, we'll have you fit." In fact, I lost weight and gained muscle, but the regimen took several weeks before Joe McDonald, a preferred training partner, said, "Look, man, you lost your gut. Now burn your pants, so you won't have anything to wear if you put it all back on again. And forget circular training: doesn't help much. Pick a large muscle group like back or shoulder. Better yet, cut out the midsection. Concentrate until you make good progress. The mirror will tell you. It never lies." I took half his advice but saved my clothes, just in case.

In the past, after a strict regimen yielding good results, I had inevitably fallen off the wagon and returned to my errant ways, with predicable results: rhino city. At the Bangkok gym, however, I daily burned my abs, pecs, and traps with renewed focus. Joe was right: both my sil-houette and raw strength improved.

JoeMac piloted helicopters in Jakarta for an American oil company. Owing to the stress factor, he worked a schedule of four on, two off throughout the year. During break he flew to Bangkok, where he trained like an Olympic athlete during the day and destroyed mind, body, and spirit in the strip clubs at night. Still under thirty, he managed to hold his own. Yet despite his magnificent physique, lean and ripped, he suffered the classic American fault: pleonexia. In *Key Largo*, Frank McCloud (played by Humphrey Bogart) confronts Johnny Rocco (played by Edward G. Robinson) and cleverly reveals his tragic flaw: "You want more." The gangster enthusiastically agrees. "That's right!" he says, laughing. "I want more."

Joe McDonald had it all: youth, health, looks, strength, and money. *Not enough.* After an exhaustive workout, we would order a health drink at the juice bar and adjourn poolside, the better to admire the topless Western women soaking up the rays. While perusing *Iron Man* magazine, Joe often remarked that with vigorous workouts, a body builder could gain the positive effects provided by steroids—namely extraordinary strength, endurance, and muscle tissue—by using natural products. A winning combination, surely, except Joe soon discovered that one could purchase performance-enhancing drugs over the counter at any pharmacy in Bangkok. Only money, a great deal on the Thai economy, was required. Like any American with a dream within reach, he took a shortcut. As a senior helicopter pilot, JoeMac commanded a handsome salary, paid in USD. Thus, a month's supply of steroids cost him a few hours' overtime in the sky. He often commented in wonder, "They actually pay me for this."

One bright afternoon, while nursing a limeade at the refreshmant stall and staring vacantly toward the pool, I noticed a silhouette making its way along the winding path toward the entrance. I thought of Lou Ferrigno, aka "The Incredible Hulk." Once out of the sun, I recognized my friend Joe, muscles bulging in protest against his custom-made silk shirt. The steroids had kicked in with a vengeance. He wasted no time in greeting. "C'mon man. Let's pump iron!"

Inside the gym, we worked in tandem—with a difference, since I helped lug extra York plates for his exercise. The weight required for each set was complemented by reps. Spotting behind the bench I would say, "Enough?", after fifteen (as opposed to the usual twelve) repetitions. "Five more," he would grunt and complete seven. Springing to his feet, we would head to the chair, where I would help him attach the wide belt with a fifty-pound plate, in order to complete twenty-five or thirty dips, take a five-second break, and mount again. Within minutes he was pumped, a weave of blood-swollen muscle, fat blue veins pulsing with each heartbeat in a sheen of perspiration. I, hands on my knees, fought to catch my breath. "Whatever you do, Joe, don't ever grow old," I said, heaving. He gave me a steady look. "Don't worry. I won't."

By his third return from Jakarta, Joe McDonald stalked the weight room like a panther on the prowl. As he moved from station to station, brave men gave him space to pump iron or leap to the pull-up bar. He posed in front of the mirror and flexed. His reflection smiled like a warrior after a successful campaign. Typical of many body builders, he tended to develop his upper torso and midsection, carving abdominals like an engraved shield. But without much effort, he created a symmetrical physique—lithe, muscular, and supple, resembling a Greek god. Tightening his quadriceps that bulged like Man o' War's sinews in the final stretch, he shook his head. "These came in the mail!" he exclaimed.

Inevitably, as the poet Houseman observed, "Glory does not stay." When he failed to keep our morning workout appointment for three days running, I made enquiry. "Oh, I heard the mirror freak is in the hospital," Rick, another weight lifter, told me. "I heard he got hepatitis from the needle." Concerned, I visited Joe in a private room, where he lay helpless on the hospital bed, surrounded by flowers contributed by his Patpong and Soi Cowboy admirers. Joe's tropical tan was replaced by a sickly jaundice hue familiar to all medical personnel in Thailand, a country infested with *Anopheles* mosquitoes.

Upon his release, looking pale and emaciated, Joe booked a flight to his home in Flatbush, the Oriental adventure over. Decades have passed since his Bangkok cameo, and Joe McDonald is no longer young. Despite best intentions, some resolves cannot be kept.

Rick, the rugger, lived for physical activity: tennis, handball, karate. However, he trained daily in the gym, not primarily to build an imposing physique like JoeMac, but to play Rugby, a British passion. Unexpectedly, he found a pitch at the famous Bangkok academy on the model of Harrow, where King Chulalongkorn's son had built an exact model, complete with an old boys' club and billiard parlor of his beloved school. Soon after arriving in fabled Siam, Rick joined the fitness center and embraced the sporting life with a vengeance, appearing at the locker room at any hour from dawn to sundown.

One morning, while reading *Time Magazine* at the juice bar, I noticed an article on the West Coast Olympic training camp. The head coach had assembled a squad of hopeful athletes and made the following proposition: "If I could guarantee a gold medal in your sport on the condition you will be dead four years later, how many would agree to this arrangement?" All hands rose as one.

Like most sensible people, I found the desire for temporary fame at literally all costs absurd. A year was a feather on the wind; four years was a slight breeze in the gale of life. Later, I mentioned the proposition to Rick, expecting him to jeer at American foolishness. Instead, he assumed a thoughtful expression. "Well, I'd think about it," he said seriously. The closing ceremony of the 1988 Olympic games occurred more than twenty-five years ago. Rick in 1988 had not celebrated his twenty-fifth birthday. Do the math.

Rick's global insurance company, based in London, had awarded him an internship in Bangkok, the better to foster international business skills as he rose through the cooperate ranks. One afternoon while I was changing in the locker room, Rick burst through the door shucking his suit jacket and loosening his tie. "Cliff, I'm glad you're here. I'm going for a personal best, and I want you to spot me." I glanced at the wall clock: well before quitting time. "Say, man, don't you keep regular office hours?" I asked. "Apparently not," he replied while modestly draping a towel around his tight midsection. "Well, what does the manager have to say about that?" I wondered aloud. "What the fuck do I care?" he answered, donning his workout shorts. "All set?" he asked. "I remembered to bring salve for our musical shoulders." We then headed for the gym, chuckling in unison.

While Rick may have been a budding eccentric, Sgt. Justin bordered on the sociopath, as first defined by Hervey Cleckley in *The Mask of Sanity*. Still, he made friends (if selectively) and enjoyed telling war stories, recounting travel adventures, and discussing philosophy, which he knew well. When feeling expansive after a workout, he would invite his training partner to join him at the hotel buffet, where, for fixed a price, famished athletes could graze with the regular herd of gourmands until quite full.

Well into his fifth decade but exceptionally fit, Justin could hold his own in the weight room. One day he said, teeth clenched, "Today I tried to bench 100 kilos and almost dropped the bar on my chest. Then I got mad and knocked off a set of five."

Justin had joined the Marines underage and first served in the occupation of Japan. He had then seen action in Korea. One boozy night, while drinking with his buddy in a Seoul dive, he had agreed to join the French Foreign Legion after discharge. In 1955, nearly broke and ready for civilian life, Justin had received a long-distance call. "Hey, buddy, I found out that we can join the Legion in Marseilles. The office is located on the coast, not in Paris like everyone thinks." Justin was in a bind. "Look, man," he said, "I haven't seen my family in years, plus I'm engaged. My fiancé will kill me." A long silence on the line. "But, Justin, you promised. . ."

A man of his word, Justin married his long-suffering girlfriend, renewed his passport, flew to Marseilles, and in North Africa endured the rigors of basic training, along with oppressive heat and sand fleas. "So how long did you play the lead in *Beau Geste*?" I enquired. "Or was it more like *Three Feathers*?" My fellow trainer, well-informed, caught the allusions and answered cryptically: "Both, plus a few more." "Well, did you speak French?" I asked. "No, but I have a smattering of German," he answered. I was taken aback. "Well, I thought the Legionnaires spoke the Gallic tongue," I said. "They do, but most of the non-coms were ex-Nazi *Fallschirmjäger*. After the war, German paratroopers who weren't imprisoned usually fled to other countries, including Argentina and America; others joined the Legion. Very well trained and used to giving orders," he added. "Well, how did you learn French?" I wondered aloud. "Pain," he answered. "The instructors figured that two commands were sufficient." He lit a cigarette and inhaled deeply. "Well, how was it at first?" I asked naïvely. "It was rough," he said. "But, you know, I like it rough." I could see that. "Did you think about packing your AWOL bag and getting your hat?" I asked. Justin laughed briefly. "More than a few times," he said. "One thing about the Legionnaires, though: If you try to desert, they understand perfectly. Very tolerant of your motives, in fact—just don't get caught!"

Justin carried his war wounds with aplomb. His left jawline, creased by a deep scar, contrasted with the dimple on his right cheek. In profile he resembled a buccaneer. The back of his neck featured a crude star formed by keloid tissue. Sensing my questions, he said, "Slashed with a *khanjar* coated with garlic in a *bedu* camp, which wasn't quite abandoned. Military intelligence, as they say, is an oxymoron. The wound putrefied within hours. My temperature spiked to 106°F, and I wrote my will in the tent that night. I was delirious and left everything to my first wife." He shook his head and chuckled. "I obviously made it, though. An Apache from my squad stole ampules of penicillin and a syringe from the clinic—which saved my ass." He moved his head from side to side, as if testing it for tight muscle. "The neck wound, bad as it looks, was superficial: a round from a sniper ricocheted off the cliff face behind me. Bled a little, but no nerve damage."

He shook his head and said with authority: "The Legionnaires are mostly outlaws, men on the run. But they look out for each other, and they're magnificent under fire. Magnificent under fire," he repeated like a prayer.

After serving five years in the Legion, he returned to the States and worked as a stringer for an underground San Francisco newspaper. Still in his early thirties, Justin had then used the GI bill to enroll in a graduate philosophy program at Stanford. Somewhat surprisingly, he had prospered. "I read in the Western canon all my life," he said. "Even in prison, when I was jailed on a passport violation, Legionnaires slipped me books." At the university, he had claimed a cordial relationship with Norman Malcolm, the Wittgenstein scholar, and said that he wrote his dissertation on Tarski, the logical positivist. I was in a position to judge intellectual posturing, and Justin maintained the learned discourse, sometimes quoting well-known terms and phrases in *Plattdeutsch*, without a slip. Although I did not press him on the matter, however, he never explained the problem of timing. Namely, how had he earned both a BA and an MA before matriculating for a doctorate at a top school while spending much of his youth in the military?

Imprinted from adolescence with the warrior code, Justin had enlisted once again to serve in Vietnam and Cambodia. After the war, he had spent most of the kick-out money during R&R in Bangkok, but had soon found that the military pension covered his living expenses. Moreover, he had married a Thai national, whose background in prostitution had prevented entry to the United States. Eventually, his passport had expired, and he had never left Sin City.

One sunny afternoon while relaxing in the corridor adjacent to the tennis court, Justin and I discussed belief systems in conjunction with medical practice. By coincidence we had both shattered bones during a parachute landing. My busted phalanges had required surgery, and after a long healing period, I had again walked and jogged without pain. Justin, who had fractured both the tibia and fibula at the ankle in Algeria, had toughed it out. A Parisian-trained medic had injected a horse tranquilizer, lined up the bones, and secured them in place with a cast. Justin had refused the surgery option, and within weeks the bones had healed. He again had marched with his squad double-time. However, in middle age, Thailand's humid climate had exacted a price: osteo-arthritis. Thus, over the years he developed a pronounced limp, exacerbated by the annual monsoon season. Although Justin could lift weights with men half his age, movement beyond a slow walk was out of the question. Still, he refused to go under the knife.

After his divorce, a Philippina masseur who provided services at the famous Cleopatra parlor had convinced him to consult a bodhisattva who presided at a *wat* in Ayutthaya, the former capital that had been destroyed by enemies in the eighteenth century and partially rebuilt. The temple, located a half-hour car ride from Krung Thep, attracted supplicants worldwide. Despite changes in government, land development, technological advances, and the influx of Western tourists, the sanctuary had retained its magic until the present day. Justin, a street-savvy world traveler, made arrangements through an influential native fixer for the healing ceremony.

The procedure itself was gratis, as practicing Buddhist clergy subsist on charity alone. Yet nothing is free, and Thailand was no exception. As expected (though actually required), Justin made a contribution at the *wat* entrance and paid the intermediary, who served as interpreter, a substantial fee for his services. A percentage of American ex-pat largesse was then passed under the table as a "gift" to the other parties.

Wat Mahathat rises majestically out of the jungle palms, and there Justin fully embraced the mysterious East. Although oriented to Western reason, well versed in logic and the scientific method, he attempted to clear his mind of epistemological pre-judgments and followed the guide past a huge, reclining Buddha to a dark enclave virtually inaccessible to curious tourists. The moist air smelled of spicy incense, which engulfed the den. Overhead, a fluttering of bats circled and swooped, on the hunt for tropical insects—a moveable feast.

Deep in the recesses of the holy *wat*, the priest, *ex cathedra*, commanded the ceremony from a teak throne, the back and arms carved with pagan symbols from the *Mahayana*. To reinforce the priest's authority, the wooden chair rested on a dais of green jade several feet above the dirt floor. The shaman, robed in white, assumed an inscrutable expression of power with humility. Thus, mise-en-scène established, the interpreter motioned to sit.

In a classic Oriental setting out of a Gothic novel, the wounded warrior underwent the *Sak Yant* cure. Stripped to the waist, Justin assumed the full lotus posture and practiced yoga breathing—a mellow, barely audible *ohm* on the exhale. But the mind is a monkey, and Justin found concentration more difficult than Marine boot camp and Legionnaire jump school. As he struggled to regain focus, a tattoo artist appeared like a specter. He opened a leather case from which he selected tools, ointment, and the dye pot—and set to work. Using a sharpened bamboo instrument, he first stimulated the *chi* by outlining a magical figure in sacred oil over the patient's solar plexus. For a permanent cure and an apotropaic, the tattooist then reworked the design with black pigment.

As a *farang* non–Buddhist, Justin was not eligible for the potent Ganesha (sacred elephant) or Garuda (eagle man), much less Hanuman, the trickster monkey god (Rama, Hanuman's master and king, had never stood a chance). The priest, in consultation with the artist, had selected an appropriate East Indian design for the occasion: a running figure that by sympathetic magic would ensure the aging athlete full recovery.

Modern tattooing has evolved since 1891, when Samuel O'Reilly patented the electric pen. The procedure, even for large, intricate pieces, is efficient and only slightly uncomfortable in most areas including arms, legs, chest, and back. The manual method, however, requires a lengthy process, painful and bloody. Breathing rhythmically, Justin concentrated on the elusive lotus blossom throughout the ordeal. "I've been through three wars, two marriages, and a goat fuck. I never cried tear one. And I've been tattooed in four continents but had to grit my teeth during this session."

Upon completion, the artist wiped the area with an oiled cloth. The tattoo glowed darkly by lantern light, whereupon the priest, speaking Pali, intoned a mantra and spat several times, the healing saliva striking the suppliant on the head and shoulders. Thus animism, shamanism, and Theravāda Buddhism combined to form a potent spell. "Arise and walk, little brother. Even run!"

In defiance of Western logic, medical science, and the common sense of Scottish philosophy, Justin's limp dissipated. While running at dawn in Lumphini Park with Khaosai Galaxy, the bantamweight champion, I heard my name. The phonemes collapsed by the Doppler effect as Justin, arms and knees pumping like a pony on parade, streaked by in a youthful sprint. Momentarily, I rejected the empirical evidence, a case of misidentification perhaps. On second glance, however, I confirmed that Justin had actually run full tilt, scores of joggers clearing the way. Although I continue to maintain a causal worldview, I now reserve a measure of skepticism when someone invokes the metaphysic of absolutes.

Don Freeland, by contrast, held no brief for Oriental folklore, mysticism, magic, or mysteries of any description. He believed in nothing but the empirical world and the cash to negotiate its labyrinths. A high school dropout, yet streetsmart since early adolescence, he had often crossed the line even when holding respectable, though dead-end jobs ranging from encyclopedia sales to pearl diving in San Francisco's Chinatown. Eventually, after warrants had been issued for petty theft and con games, he had turned fugitive and headed south. Desperate for ready cash, he had dealt drugs in Los Angeles for nearly a year, and after taking his considerable cut, he had bought plane tickets for a world tour.

He had not traveled far. After a lost weekend in The Kangaroo Club, which had featured oral sex as the patron quaffed a cold Singha beer at the bar, he had decided (like veterans, tourists, and pilgrims in search of Oriental wisdom and enlightenment) to stay indefinitely. In fact, the Land of Smiles offered sex, drugs, seafood, custom clothes, tropical temperatures, travel opportunities, and other delights for small change. The people were relaxed, friendly, and tolerant. Generally, Thais found human peccadilloes amusing, rather than the usual opportunity to judge and punish. If, for example, a married woman discovered that her husband made frequent visits to the notorious massage/sex parlors with his friends, *mai pen rai*—so long as he observed his responsibilities as provider and parent, paid the rent, and carried on his extra-marital affairs with discretion and dignity.

Thus, after first sampling Bangkok's cultural buffet, legal or otherwise, without censure or serious threat to general well-being, Don Freeland found his destiny, ironically, in Muang Thai [Freeland] and threw the plane tickets, worth thousands, in the trash. He had soon married a Soi Cowboy pole dancer and settled in a rental home within walking distance of Sukhumvit. Gainful employment was never a consideration. Don was twenty-six, however, and strong as a cobra. He soon grew restless. As a student of the martial arts and an accomplished street fighter, he made arrangements through a taxi driver (a former boxer) to take lessons in *Muay Thai*, the national sport, in the Khlong Toei slum. However, the training was rigorous and exhausting, which required additional preparation in the gym, where he pumped iron, stretched, and strengthened his midsection for several hours each morning. After a brief nap and a blender fruit drink, he reported to the outdoor training area for lessons.

His body language and expression, which John described accurately as "something between a sneer and a grimace" forestalled casual conversation. He rarely spoke beyond a perfunctory grunt in passing. I paid little attention to a fellow American who preferred his own company, until one day I noticed that his stretching exercises indicated past karate training. Curious, I asked him about his background in the martial arts. "Yeah," he said grunting, "I studied under Norris and earned a second-degree brown belt. I wanted to finish, but I had 'to take care of business.'" I understood the bland euphemism, which could mean anything from fulfilling a contract by a hit man to enforcing a drug deal. In response, I mentioned that, while living in Columbus, Ohio, I had competed on the open circuit after earning a Shodan in Kenpo under the direction of Jay T. Will, who had taught me private lessons twice a week for several years. Don turned his head to make eye contact and said knowingly. "Well, Jay Will is serving time in the federal pen." I caught my breath. "What for? Assault?" I asked. "Drug dealing," Don replied.

By my mid-forties I had witnessed public beheadings, live sex shows on the Deuce, the aftermath of a bloody suicide, an orgy in full swing, several barroom brawls, attempted arson, and as in the advertising tagline, "much much more." Yet I felt a jolt like electricity at his casual statement. "I find that hard to believe," I said firmly. "I have known Jay since 1970, and he doesn't drink or smoke. He takes a dim view of drugs and as a matter of fact, when I showed for my black belt test, he said I couldn't take it. When I protested, he said a couple of dojo groupies had told him that I had stopped by their apartment recently and smoked pot, so I was automatically disqualified. Since we were friends, and I had published a number of articles on karate, he gave in, but he wasn't happy about it." Don stood and loosened up. "Well," he insisted, "that's the word on the street."

Don was correct. To pay down debt, Jay had contacted a fellow martial arts instructor with connections to the Cuban mafia. Jay had agreed to act as middleman and had soon cleared the debt and made a profit. Greed prevailed over good sense, however, and through an informant anxious to plea bargain, the DEA had learned that Jay was selling coke out of his dojo. With a preponderance of evidence, the feds had eventually arrested Jay on felony charges. The judge had ruled that despite Jay Will's clean record and outstanding reputation as a role model, he had solely been motivated by greed. Consequently, Jay T. Will, in the prime of life, had faced eight years in the federal penitentiary. Owing to health problems, however, he was later released on probation after serving approximately four years. In 1996, the celebrated sensei died of heart failure at fifty-three.

Despite our differing views on selling/using illegal drugs, Don and I bonded on our mutual interests in training, the martial arts, and boxing. Each Saturday after our workout, we took a taxi to "Dick's Tiger Den" in the notorious Bangkok area called Patpong. The head bartender and co-owner, Richard "the Bread Man" Dougherty, had earned legendary status as a Navy SEAL during the Vietnam conflict. After discharge, Dick had headed to Sin City for extended R&R. With his Thai wife to sign the documents and hard cash for a down payment, he had bought the bar and decorated it with war memorabilia: framed medals; personal letters from SEAL team members along with testimonies from American, British, Vietnamese military personnel; and signed photographs by celebrities such as Gene Hackman and George Foreman, fat and smiling like a friendly insurance salesman.

Word spread of the Patpong Mecca. Ex-SEALs and active-duty mercs, grunts, special ops, Rangers, Delta Forces, Legionnaires, and allied commandos arrived in droves. The decorated and wounded warriors, along with unfledged new recruits, privates, sleeves, and wannabes, made pilgrimages to share war stories and a few pops with the Bread Man. No poseur was turned away, but few left sober.

Unlike the regulars at the Den, however, Don and I expressed no interest in free drinks, nude dancing, or live sex shows—the latter exhibitions easily available at nearby establishments—touted by the scantily clad waitresses who were eager for tips or other profitable arrangements. Seated at a well-padded booth adjacent to the bar, we ordered soft drinks and watched TV.

For an added draw, Dick ran "Iron Mike" Tyson matches, starting from his amateur bouts to the unblemished early round victories in mid-career, all for the price of a great big cold orange Fanta for *batseep* [80] *baht* a glass, plus small change for the smiling bargirls, who, when not dancing *sans* costume on the nearby stage, hovered nearby like hummingbirds, attentive to every whim.

The atmosphere, lively but not threatening, fairly crackled with testosterone. During the weekend Happy Hour, which started Friday afternoon and extended until the last forward observer staggered toward the exit the following Sunday morning, one might have expected conception without the usual formalities at the Tiger Den.

A charged atmosphere proved infectious, and the ambience alone produced a contact high. Don offered insightful comments on the boxing matches, as one opponent after the next struggled to remain upright under the remorseful blows by Iron Mike. During a long round, while a stocky fighter absorbed a harvest of straight jabs, uppercuts, and left hooks, Don remarked grimly, "Right now, he *hates* boxing."

I am conversant in the sweet science and trained briefly under Danny "Lou Lou" Perez, the middleweight, when my high school friend Rudy Pavesi prepared for his first preliminary match against Chuck "The Bayonne Bleeder" Wepner in Madison Square Garden. Over the years I have attended a number of contests in New York City and Teaneck, New Jersey, plus I have read Oates, Liebling, Hauser, Ward, Remnick, Fried, et al., along with "told to" autobiographies by many of the great fighters. Don, however, had achieved encyclopedic knowledge in the sport: from the pugilistic skills of Irish immigrants to the Golden Age of the early twentieth-century fighters to staying current with the second renaissance of the seventies, when Forman, Frazier, Norton, and the great Mohammed Ali had brought boxing to new standards of courage, endurance, and excellence.

One afternoon while witnessing still another contender hit the canvas, Don said, "You know, in golf, basketball, soccer, tennis, and baseball, you can have a bad day. In boxing, it might mean the end of your career."

Don nearly ended his nefarious career by returning to Los Angeles in order to settle a business arrangement, which involved collecting on an outstanding debt. The gentleman in arrears refused to pay, and Mr. Freeland bypassed the legal process by executing a spear-hand strike, which detached the man's retina, followed by a roundhouse kick that fractured two ribs. While the welcher strugged to regain his feet, Don popped the defenseless opponent with his elbow, a vicious temple strike that drew blood. Meanwhile, the victim's wife, an eyewitness from her apartment window, called 911. An open and shut case. While awaiting trial, a disgruntled associate connected Don with a recent drug bust, a revelation which meant a stiff jail sentence. During straight time, Don managed, in Thai fashion, to flee the scene. He flew to Chiang Mai, where he made arrangements with his mother-in-law, who (as mentioned) had established a duck farm on a property he had purchased the previous year. He maintained his drug habit at a nearby Akha village, where, so long as a visitor remained in the community, he or she could smoke opium with impunity.

Don briefly returned to Bangkok and stopped by the fitness center to say goodbye. I never saw Don Freeland—drug dealer, boxing *aficionado*, street fighter, and duck farmer—again.

In due time, I also left Bangkok and eventually found work in other foreign countries, where I certainly met interesting people and formed lasting friendships, but no experience overseas ever quite matched my daily encounters at the Bangkok Fitness Center in the Land of the Lotos Eaters.

IV.

Casting Pearls

The sun will not overstep his measures; if he does, the
Erinyes, the hand-maids of Justice, will find him out.
—Heraclitus

Jeff Hickson, my friend and colleague, could be described as a good
old boy with a PhD in Medieval literature and university wit. "We are
a couple of aging scholars washed up on the shoals of Asia Minor," he
observed, adding, "and this is no country for old men." Another Dr.
Hickson insight: "We have a job, but it's not a career."

Those and similar pronouncements were issued from the Bilkent
campus, located approximately six miles from the Turkish capital,
which boasted two animal species: humans and pigeons. Owing to
heavy pollution, one was not plagued by insects or repulsed by ver-
min attracted to filth and squalor. The City of Knowledge's (Turkish
translation of "Bilkent") topography, on the other hand, provided a
modest bird sanctuary. Tiny boreal owls, whose plumage perfectly
matched the battleship-grey light posts where they roosted by day,
glided into the surrounding meadows on the hunt. An unkindness of
ravens, snow-white, appeared magically from the nearby pine forest to
feast on kitchen supplies, which I had unwisely set on the balcony
while cleaning the fridge. Otherwise, like phantoms, the ghostly birds
disappeared.

But thieves in the bushes proved the least of my concerns at Bilkent,
a beautiful campus still under construction when I arrived in fall of
1991 with great expectations, two pieces of luggage, and a new electric typewriter. Within a few weeks, I had discovered that the entire
university enterprise rested on a joke, and he who laughed last was

the last one to appreciate the punch line: get with the program or pay the piper. Given the schizoid, Byzantine ethos practiced by the academic community there, the above mixed metaphor was appropriate.

The Bilkent GOGWAR ("great old game without any rules") was easily described: "Our Benefactor" (the preferred title conferred on the Turkish Trump, who had both built and owned the school) decreed no required entrance exam in the school charter. That unusual practice attracted hordes of degree candidates or rather their *nouveau riche* parents, who paid tuition fees on the American scale. Thus, the difference in educational systems: according to the traditional European model, not everyone was deemed worthy of higher learning, and consequently, on passing a stiff examination, the degree-earning process cost a pittance, whereas according to the American model, virtually everyone was entitled to a degree, but at a considerable price. Bilkent operated on the US plan, strictly applied, since government grants or scholarships at the City of Knowledge were not obtainable.

Bilkent culture, an extension of the political model, was grounded on corruption. Specifically, those who paid and tarried for the requisite terms were awarded a degree, regardless. We looked to the Dodo's pronouncement in *Alice's Adventures in Wonderland* for the university credo: "Everybody has won, and all must have prizes." Therein lies the conundrum. Given the fact that not all intelligent people are able to learn from books, a certain percentage of candidates were bound to fail—just as some athletes are not able to run a mile under four minutes. We were stating an absolute, existential fact with no exceptions. Three problems remained: required tests, written assignments, and final exams.

Unexpectedly, those scholars who were slow and steady, but could not possibly win the race (since "slow" and "win" in that context was a classic oxymoron) were eventually graduated from Bilkent in any case. Solution: cheat!

As I have good reason to know, human beings tend to borrow passages without acknowledgment. Literary history confirms that a number of illustrious writers, scholars, and world leaders have been caught with their hands in the cookie jar. As a case in point, the Four Last Things sermon in *Portrait of the Artist* is not the author's writing. Yet although some cultures are more tolerant of fudging than others, academic dishonesty remains, in theory, universally forbidden, and those who transgress face consequences. Doubtless, no one holds a brief for plagiarism, ghost writing, sharing answers, and similar unethical practices at the City of Knowledge.

Likewise, only the clinically deranged would argue seriously that American citizens are entitled to violate gun laws, but the difference between legislation, practice/political speeches, and strict enforcement could be described as a wide gulf. According to the strong misreading of the Second Amendment, the NRA and their bought minions fiercely argue that virtually everyone should be armed under most any circumstances, period. "No one is going to take away our guns!" is an American shibboleth, uttered in tones of barely-controlled rage, self-righteousness, and threat.

In Turkey, the practice of cheating was not simply widespread but endemic. Tactics ranged from outright plagiarism to distracting the male professor with tight, well-filled sweaters. Students, speaking Turkish argot, shared information with one another during tests. They sometimes acquired (i.e., stole) exam questions and looked up the answers beforehand. The occasional well-prepared student wrote essays for money, sexual favors, or simply goodwill. Quite literally: no end to it.

But surely, someone must have objected to a practice that, from the standpoint of acquiring knowledge and intellectual skills, undercut the educational system? In certain instances, my intrepid, high-paid colleagues did finally call attention to the fact: a pristine student essay, for instance, that had first appeared as Harold Bloom's introduction to *The Awakening* in the Chelsey House edition. Due process, basically observed in the breach under most circumstances, had to be followed to the letter at Bilkent. Briefly put, an *ad hoc* committee, minus the faculty accuser, decided the matter, and invariably the miscreant was entitled to a makeup. Despite the annoying delay, however, which was not encouraged by the Chair or dean, no one in the short history of the college ever failed the given course. I never learned the rule-bending sleight of hand involved, but I stand by the statement.

The semester began not with a bang, but a whimper. My over-subscribed class in English Renaissance met well before noon, and more than a few of the young scholars were hung-over, since carousing at Marilyn's, a popular Americanized bar, defeated class preparation. As a considerate gesture to student priorities, the university ran two buses, twenty minutes apart, from campus to Ankara 9:00 a.m. to midnight. One load of roisterers was delivered to the corner less than one block from Marylin's; the other bus dropped off eager consumers, credit cards at the ready, near the department stores, with bars conveniently located in the area for the parched shoppers.

The two sections of American literature (surveys: Prose Fiction from Irving to Melville and Transcendental Poets) barely made a quorum; the students slouched sullenly in their seats, dying for a smoke. I ignored the hostile stares from those scholars who were not napping and held forth, instead, with enthusiasm until the fifteen-minute break, when the mob came to life and stampeded to light up in the smoke-filled hallway.

As a youth, I had smoked Camels, the richest and best-tasting cigarette, made with Turkish tobacco. That processed weed, which kills more civilians than cluster bombs, remains the favored drug throughout the country of its origin. An alarming percentage of Turkish young people lose one or both parents before their majority. Presumably, those reckless drivers who are not killed on the road die of lung cancer and related diseases in early middle age.

After a two-week monologue on various topics, including the function of allegory in *Volpone*, the Great Chain of Being, chronotope in "Young Goodman Brown," and biblical allusions in Whitman, I gave a spot quiz in all three classes. During each test, I noticed a distinct rumbling in Turkish—to me, a foreign language beyond greetings, directions, and ordering kabobs. I had written, "No talking during the test" on the whiteboard and repeated that directive several times while the students scribbled their hearts out. The correct answers, nevertheless, were remarkably similar, three out of three—or the entire class had cheated.

As a gesture to cultural relativism, a common excuse for barbaric behavior like stoning women who had misbehaved sexually (though it takes two to tango) in certain Muslim countries, I simply nullified the tests and explained patiently the "rules" of scholarship, borrowing a line from *Raging Bull*: cheating "defeats its whole purpose!" I cast too few pearls for satisfactory results. The students continued to employ any means, fair or foul, to pass exams and submit acceptable assignments. The lines were drawn; it was war.

I then consulted my veteran colleagues, who had dealt, after a fashion, with wholesale cheating as well—each according to his or her own perspective. The various positions were astonishing: "It's their degree, which is worthless, so let them hang themselves"; "Given the job market in the States, I was lucky to land this post, which pays well"; and even "They don't call Turkey 'the sick man of Europe' for no reason."

Yet Dr. Benani, a junior instructor, claimed after more than three years at Bilkent, he had never encountered cheating problems. I was baffled, since my associate was certainly competent, sensible, and as a tough Texan, quite savvy. We taught the same students, so the odds of radical difference in behavior approached zero. Moreover, no one, including the young scholars themselves, denied that cheating occurred during exams. For several weeks I pondered the mystery and reluctantly concluded that my colleague must have been lying through his teeth. But I was mistaken.

By an unexpected coincidence that has informed my entire life, the administration assigned me, a senior faculty member, to audit Professor

Benani's course in Victorian literature and report my findings to the American/British Promotion (only) Committee, tenure being off-limits to foreign faculty members. I immediately advised my colleague that I expected to attend the next class meeting and informed him that I would take notes. I felt no surge of anticipation; surely, after decades on both sides of the lectern, I had little to learn about pedagogical method. I had begun college teaching in 1963, soon after my own graduation, later holding faculty positions at some half-dozen universities in America and abroad. By 1991, I'd seen it all—or so I thought.

On the day of reckoning, I found the students were unusually quiet, well behaved, and alert. Dr. Benani wrote the entire lesson on the whiteboard. Understandable, since the academic register sometimes disoriented conscientious native speakers, let alone those who were barely literate in a second language. A written lecture was unusual, certainly, but I missed the gimmick. Human psychology cannot be explained like a geometric proof, but radical disjunction, without the threat of lethal force or promise of exceptional reward, simply does not occur. Group behavior operates according to self-interest, especially when negative reinforcement is not a factor. When, however, a few weeks later, I served as monitor during my colleague's midterm exam, I understood. The students were instructed to comment on three (out of five) essay questions, an open note book test. The queries, of course, corresponded closely to written material already provided by the professor. Grades ranged from B+ to A+. Technically, no cheating had occurred, so Dr. Benani had spoken the truth. A codicil, however, is indicated to round out the pedagogical caper.

Upper-class students were permitted to apply directly for admission two or three days before classes began. I arrived early and waited patiently, reading at my desk, for students eager to profit by my tutelage. None appeared. I twice checked the schedule for time and place, which matched. Still, no anxious students to say, "I hope I'm able to sign up for your lectures, sir." Meanwhile, I noticed familiar faces in twos or threes passing my open door without a nod, a smile, or a wave. Curious, I stepped into the hall and blinked. The line stretched at least thirty feet outside Dr. Benani's office. Patient applicants included middle-aged women (mothers), whose children (off some-where) had instructed their doting parent to sign them up for *any* course under Professor Benani's direction. Without fail those parents waited patiently in line.

But my ordeal lay ahead. At some point, one of my Turkish colleagues mentioned that my English literature students all expected to gradu-ate in June. The surplus number of Renaissance scholars proved to be no accident: the survey, a required course, had not been offered for two years. I knew by then that Byzantine bureaucracy was not informed by Teutonic efficiency, and I girded my loins for the struggle ahead. Despite my best-laid plans, at term's end, as surely as night fol-lows day, catastrophe occurred: mine, theirs, and the administration's. All three parties found themselves, at different levels, in the deep weeds. Specifically, the students confronted disgrace; the administra-tion felt compromised; and I was odd man out, facing, like the film heroine abducted by a silverback in heat, "a fate worse than death"— two years, the standard sentence, in a Turkish prison.

In assigning the required term paper, I had worded the particulars broadly: "Submit a five-page (minimum) essay on some aspect of Renaissance literature and/or culture with adequate documentation. Your thesis should be informed by an appropriate methodology of your choice." Plenty of scope, I thought, with little opportunity for plagiarism, since I could easily distinguish student expression from, say, an analysis by Stephen Greenblatt. I calculated correctly, but only in a strict, technical sense. The first paper, though not polished prose, met the requirements for a B paper: seven typed pages, logical struc-ture, clear thesis, passable diction, syntax, and punctuation. Smiling inwardly, I declared victory—until I read the second essay. The expres-sion differed slightly, but the formal elements did not. The third, fourth, etc. followed the identical pattern and so on *ad nauseam*.

The explanation was obvious: a template composition, equally distrib-uted by way of the photocopy machine, provided all the necessary fac-tors save precise wording. Not exactly plagiarism in the absolute sense, but close enough, since I had specifically included "acknowledge with end notes ideas not your own" in my definition of academic dishonesty, which was clearly written and later explained in some detail. "Too late to say you're sorry, shipmates." I failed the entire senior class, submitted the incriminating documents, along with my final grades to the executive assistant, and traveled by bus to Damascus with a British-born, Arabic-speaking friend from the English Language Division. By coincidence I had known Moodie slightly while in Riyadh, and we had unexpectedly met again in Athens over summer break. Ten years later, we both taught, though in different departments, at Bilkent.

While exploring the sprawling *Al-Hamidiyah Souq*, a labyrinth of shops and stalls smelling of fresh fruit, homemade sweets, leather, and sandalwood, I gave little thought to Bilkent, Ankara, or Turkey itself. As for my Renaissance students, let them follow Voltaire's sage advice and cultivate, each by each, his or her own garden.

....

Upon my return, I checked the mail in the faculty lounge to find, along with several personal letters and the usual notices, a rude summons to report, ASAP, to the Chair's office. No reason given, but I could make an educated guess: The students had, in my absence, raised bloody hell about their well-deserved grades. Without passing the British survey course, which was not again offered until fall semester, no one would graduate. All that Turkish lira, all that time drinking at Marilyn's, all those ingenious schemes to pass the required course—wasted.

Entering the smoke-filled room after a light knock, I opened with a quip: "We ought to hang a couple of hams in here." Dr. Bozkurt inhaled, grunted a polite greeting, and let my witticism pass. She did not waste time on pleasantries, but cut to the chase. "Your Renaissance students are quite upset." I sighed, barely feigning sympathy for the cheats, much less for the Chair's plight. She might have handled the outraged scholars, but incensed parents were quite another matter. Moreover, the school President and his aggressive wife did not practice a hands-off policy during student crises. Promotions, salaries, contracts, careers—all on the line.

"I gave them fair warning and in writing," I replied. Ignoring my defense, she went on to say that, unless we could come to some arrangement, all concerned were in for an unpleasant time. (The long pause) "I strongly suggest a make-up," she stated predictably. "I don't give make-ups without proof of broken bones, catastrophic illness, or pregnancy," I said firmly. With the subtlety of a Midwest tornado, the Chair then drew her Ace in the hole: the *Godfather* offer I could not refuse. If I insisted on failing the entire class, she said, the matter would be referred to the High Court in Ankara. Unstated, but strongly implied, a jail sentence might well be imposed.

I remembered a scene from *A Flag for Sunrise*. The novel, set in a banana republic included an aggrieved character who threatened the protagonist with legal action, adding that he would not like prison. "The food is terrible. God knows if they have even heard of lobster Newburg." Bad food did not concern me; I could have afforded to lose a few pounds. However, I had read *Midnight Express*, and I did not want to add the dreaded *falaka* [lashing the soles of the feet] to my overseas experiences. Moreover, I knew the difference between the priceless and the worthless, and my physical "integrity" (as T.E. Lawrence delicately wrote about the sexual assault by Turkish soldiers) was a clear example of the former. I recalled an old hand who had said, "If sentenced in Turkey, give your soul to Jesus, because Mehmet with have your ass." Thus, dismissal (or some other minor penalty from the diploma mill known as the "City of Knowledge") for doing my job hardly registered as more than a minor inconvenience.

Yet as an American citizen with a pristine academic/personal record, I did not feel entirely vulnerable. My checkered career had never flourished, plus I had achieved solvency without debt, dependents, or vices. Finally, as a former street fighter, parachutist, SCUBA diver, and black-belt competitor, feckless administrators given to threats did not easily intimidate me.

I said nothing in reply and left her majesty's office. To cover my bets, however, I bought a one-way ticket home and packed an AWOL bag. Like the Mailer character in "The Man Who Studied Yoga," I kept my eye on the door. A few of my close friends, including my traveling companion Mahmoud Hourani, expressed indignation. Two colleagues, in fact, wrote letters to Our Benefactor on my behalf. The expressions of support went unanswered. Meanwhile, the High Court—a familiar institution out of *The Trial*—made endless demands: syllabus, sample exams, grade scale, and so on. One day an officer of the court called to request an essay test, written by me. "I administer exams; I don't take them anymore." He went silent for long seconds. "Ah, but you must."

"Judo" means the "gentle way": that is, *technique* in the martial art trumps *physical strength*. Consequently, a skillful older man might easily throw an impulsive, muscular youngster by redirecting energy. In like fashion, after each question, I listed the most arcane, technical, abstruse jargon in several languages (including French, German, and Russian) known to me after decades of studying, lecturing, publishing, and discussing literary theory. I used terms associated with philosophy, linguistics, anthropology, and psychology with no consideration for context, logic, or coherence—all grist for the mill. I knew that the court consultants would be loath to reveal their abysmal ignorance, since my Turkish colleagues, by and large, could barely analyze *The Good Earth* using Anglo-American formalism, much less provide an interpretation of *Pale Fire* by employing Kisteva's intertextuality. Predictably, I never heard from the officer of the Court again.

After weeks of one-way correspondence with the Ankara legal system: nothing. The semester progressed without incident. The cheating problem receded to manageable levels. In practice, I would confront the suspect student, who often admitted to the fault. I would then notify the Chair in writing that he or she would fail the course. No response from anyone involved.

At the start of second semester a young woman in my fall term American Literature class requested a make-up final. She had recently given birth. I remembered her condition from the last semester and agreed. Weary of nonsense, I set give-away questions, e.g., "Describe Claggart's obsession with Billy Budd. Provide concrete details." With minimal background in Melville's novella and less thought, even a mediocre student might have earned an automatic C. The woman's answers, however, were unusually sophisticated and more importantly, did not address the questions. Obviously, her classmates had provided a learned discussion from *their* final, and she had memorized the material. I awarded her an F.

For perseverance, she deserved an A. She offered a range of arguments, like a ward heeler begging for votes. Her appeals ranged from demands to sophistry to outright pleading. To her credit she did not attempt the old chestnut: "Sir, I would do *anything* to pass this course!" Finally, she exhausted all known (as well as some original) appeals. "Professor Hallam, you are a hard man." Like a well-rehearsed actor, I replied on cue, "Yes, and the longer I stay in Turkey, the harder I get." I sent a memo to the Chair and heard nothing more.

The Dean, who remained in his office during the ongoing farce, issued a terse letter to the effect that I had not notified the university of my trip to Damascus over break, and I should make arrangements to leave so as to avoid last-minute problems. Given the fact that mindless bureaucracy informed the system, from misaddressing the acceptance letter to losing my work permit to issuing a bogus ATM card to misplacing a textbook order, I appreciated his concern.

Otherwise, the semester passed uneventfully. No student uprisings, no summons to the Chair's plush office, no additional requests from the High Court in Ankara. On the day before my departure, the administrative office notified me of a delay in processing my exit visa. I did not protest, and the secretary sighed with relief. Evidently, I had earned a reputation as having a short temper. I decided to wait while bureaucrats frantically searched file cabinets. Unexpectedly, Dr. Bozkurt made a grand entrance, smoke streaming from both nostrils. "The Court ruled in your favor," she announced. "Since you included a warning on each handout and exam, the notification of penalty served as a contract." I said nothing, glanced at my watch. The Chair made an abrupt exit. "Another day, another lawsuit," I murmured. Yet

I did not feel at ease until I cleared customs. Like Joseph K. in Kafka's *The Trial*, I had come to believe that the Court and its agents were ubiquitous, impossible to avoid or escape.

But my Byzantine adventure continued. After passing an interview at Födz University in the Turkish Republic of North Cyprus, I signed a two-year contract to teach graduate seminars in linguistics and literature with full freedom to create the given course. The salary, to be paid in Sterling, proved more than adequate, along with a spacious, well-furnished apartment. Home free! Before the summer session had ended, however, I had learned to appreciate the expression "out of the frying pan and into the fire."

V.

The Groves of Academus

Such, such were the joys. . . .
And sport no more seen,
On the darkening Green.
—Blake, "The Echoing Green"

Födz University—like all great institutions—was founded on a vision, a City on a Hill. The late twentieth-century construction site, a virtual beehive of industry, hovered on a gentle rise above a grassy meadow, where Turkish paratroopers had landed during the 1974 invasion of Cyprus. The Greek possession, named after ancient copper mines long depleted like the rain forest felled to build the Roman fleet, served as the world's navel, attracting disparate marauders such as Hittite armies, Egyptian pharaohs, and Arab warlords. Throughout the centuries, Cyprus had played host to a number of celebrities, including Odysseus, St. Paul, and Rimbaud. The island, according to long tradition, had even provided an altar for St. Nicholas, aka Santa Claus.

In the middle 1970s, the Turkish military had seized the day during a Greek officer coup and struck. Quickly overcoming token resistance from poorly armed and unprepared citizens, the mainland warriors had consequently divided the island, pushing the longtime Greek residents south and awarding the northern portion to their countrymen, who had then taken possession of the villas, gardens, small cities, and seaports on the blue/green Mediterranean. Many new landlords, restaurateurs, shop owners, and the like had promptly sold or leased their windfall properties to entrepreneurs throughout the world, thus making promised *Enosis* [union], a pipe dream of opportunistic politicians, a promise that to this day had never been kept. A superficial glance at the political/legal circumstances confirms that such a union would require a legal exercise in casuistry required of attorneys in the case of Jarndyce vs. Jarndyce.

My interest in the island did not center on Near East politics or recent historical events, but in bookish pursuits: namely an enquiry into canonical texts from the classics to postmodernism, from traditional criticism to modern hermeneutics. A position at Födz U., assuming I passed the interview(s), would number my eighth post, all told, since the beginning of my unorthodox career in the fall of 1963. My recent faculty position at Bilkent University on the mainland had come to an abrupt end owing to a cheating scandal, the final straw, which had eliminated the entire fourth year class from the commencement ceremonies and me from the faculty at the academic year's end.

The news of my imminent departure spread, and soon after receiving the terse letter of dismissal, a friendly colleague married to a Cypriot national passed along the Födz University job notice and advised me to apply. "On Cyprus, they will treat you right," he assured me. Call me naïve, call me an innocent babe in the woods if you will, but I believed my learned friend and mailed a *billet-doux*, along with my resume to the Department of Literature. Two days later, a Dr. Bugra called my office and invited me for an interview: "to make arrangements for mutual benefit." I did so the same day.

Thus, leaving on short notice from Bilkent, I had not prepared well for a vigorous interrogation during one or more interviews for the position of Associate Professor as advertised in the university newsletter. Nevertheless, confidence overcame anxiety in the matter. By then in my early fifties, a well rehearsed veteran of oral examinations, convention presentations, lively classroom exchanges, plus dorm/bar/coffee house disputes in America and abroad, I could discuss literary matters off the cuff with aplomb.

Arriving in late afternoon at the north Cyprus airport, I passed easily through customs and noticed a tall figure with an alabaster face peering like a spectral ivory tower over various diminutive greeters, some holding signs advertising rooms and transportation. It was Professor Gul (Rose) Bugra, Head of Department at Födz U. As I approached, she leaned toward me, "Doctor Hallam?" Gul asked, looking apprehensive. "Yes, I'm all set. Just this Gladstone," I answered, glancing toward my hand luggage. She nodded and turned. "My car is parked behind the taxi stand," she said, leading the way.

On the road to the university, Gul made light conversation. She drove expertly with one hand, holding a cigarette in the other. The departmental complex, located a few feet from the basement snack bar, consisted of several cluttered rooms, all empty, except for a secretary busily typing as we passed into the Chair's modest office. We sat opposite one another, only a few feet apart. Gul lit a cigarette and inhaled deeply. Neither of us spoke. Glancing about the room, I noticed a plaque with an imposing fortress bristling with armaments; the legend in Turkish proclaimed Bacon's statement "Knowledge is Power" in bold letters. I turned to Dr. Bugra with an expectant expression, ready for questions.

From an administrative standpoint, the interview proved a dismal failure. Yet I passed brilliantly. After several false starts that led to nothing of substance punctuated by long, awkward silences, I finally understood that I was expected to provide both the questions and the answers. As a graduate friend had described his oral examination for a doctorate in Medieval Studies: "A piece of cake!" To ease Gul's evident embarrassment, I rehearsed a personal incident in which an attractive job candidate whose knowledge did not match her appearance made me a tempting offer on the ride back to her hotel. Gul smiled slightly. I then asked if she had "any more questions," irony being my favorite rhetorical device.

Satisfied with my impromptu performance, Gul suggested we adjourn to the President's office, located in a nearby not-quite-completed building. Like Mussolini, the university CEO had promoted a sense of grandeur by minimally furnishing the spacious room with two straight-back chairs. President Avic's immense desk, bare of documents, dwarfed His Eminence, who appeared child-like in the huge chair made of polished walnut with padded arm rests. Mr. Avic greeted me warmly and motioned for us to be seated. Gul provided a brief introduction, which we acknowledged with a nod and eye contact.

"Well," he said brightly, "you have noticed that we Cypriots are more friendly than people on the mainland." I cleared my throat. "How much did they pay you in Ankara?" he demanded. I quoted my salary in Turkish lira. "Födz offers more, in pounds Sterling," he added. "We treat our faculty like family here." I attempted a witty reply. "Well, I prefer bitter lemons to sour grapes," I quipped. He glanced at Gul for a positive signal and turned to me. "Did you see the dorm under construction at the end of the main drive?" he asked. "Yes," I answered, "everyone is very busy." He nodded. "The excavation to the left," he went on, "will be the swimming pool. The biggest one on the island—even larger than the Olympic pool in Morphou," he added triumphantly. I noted that he tended to confuse the intelligible with the sensible, but I smiled in agreement. Reminiscing about the future, he predicted that our colleagues from nearby universities would maneuver for an invitation to visit by the pool on a hot summer's day.

Abruptly, he then narrowed his eyes slightly and spoke with authority. "If you don't agree to stay more than one year," he said, "we won't accept." I returned his gaze. "Offer me a two-year contract," I countered, "and I'll sign." Ignoring my response, he announced a weekly shoptalk gathering in Girna, lubricated by *ouzo*. I gave my stock answer to cocktail party invitations: "I quit drinking after I married." Avic turned pale and stared vacantly for long seconds. "Except," I added, "for special occasions, of course."

Color returned to his blue jowls as he announced his generous offer. "Summer school seminar for MA students in linguistics. Half pay. Do you accept?" I hesitated and replied, "Well, my field is literature and linguistics is a topic with a wide range of specialized areas. But I do have knowledge of the subject. I know something about semantics, syntax, morphology—the basics. I'm also well-grounded in structuralism, which is important for literary theory." He looked pleased. "Just give them a good background," he exclaimed. Turning to Gul, he said, "Show Doctor Hallam his furnished flat—free with the contract," he added.

University housing, within easy walking distance of the campus, did not disappoint: a large, clean, well-lighted place: spacious kitchen and dining area, nice living room, bathtub with shower, comfortable bed flanked by a walk-in closet, and small study with a wide bookcase flanking the far wall. At my request, the administration provided a large TV in order to watch the summer Olympics. I was allowed long-distance calls and charged them to the school. Soon after getting settled, I sent a dozen or so postcards featuring Othello's castle on the sea to family, friends, and former colleagues.

I met my first class composed of young adults, some married. They greeted me as I entered, a sheaf of papers in hand. After opening statements concerning attendance, grading policy, and penalties for academic dishonesty—plagiarism, in particular—I announced a short quiz. "In order to determine the level of material we will discuss in this class, I would like you to provide a working definition of basic terms, anonymously. The tests will not be graded; the information is simply for my own use." Two graduate students in linguistics correctly defined "semantics" as "word meaning," and the rest turned in blank pages. One scholar, I am certain, copied from the other. The small exercise in competence and academic honesty set the tone for the rest of the summer session.

Using an introductory textbook, better suited for undergraduates seeking humanities credits, I required my students to learn the phonetic alphabet and within a few sessions diagram sentences for deep structure. We went on to reflexive pronouns and idiomatic expressions. All but a young army veteran named Attila, a strapping young man better suited to orchard work (the family business) than intellectual pursuits, barely managed to follow the lessons, respond correctly in class, and complete outside assignments—which were neither difficult nor lengthy. At summer's end, the slow learner barely passed the final exam, but I fudged his grade to a B-. I hoped for his GPA and my piece of mind our professor/student relationship was over. Attila was not, in New Jersey parlance, "college material."

And so my brief tenure at Födz U. began. The daily schedule settled into a rhythm: a short walk to campus followed by an hour to collect/read my correspondence, a cursory glance at my lecture notes followed by ninety minutes of uninterrupted explanations in order to give the scholars a "good background," as Avic had suggested. Not a bad gig, and the salary proved more than sufficient for my modest needs.

The necessities of everyday life—including laundry, transportation, entertainment, and nourishment—posed no problem. I often ate a fresh fish dinner at one of the Girna restaurants with outside tables located a few feet from the water. For several weeks, in fact, I regularly savored delectable and inexpensive seafood dishes, better enjoyed on occasion by uninvited guests, who stopped by my table to chat. The natives were friendly and civil. Many took a surprisingly liberal, tolerant, and even generous view of the chronic political crisis. None made insulting or disparaging comments about the Greeks, who occupied the southern portion of the island.

I continued the immovable feast on the bounty of the sea until one day I read an alarming article in the English language newspaper: Scientists had determined that the Mediterranean, though deceptively beautiful, was not harmless. In fact, the waters were heavily polluted, and the toxins, a product of industrial waste by several countries, were being absorbed by the fish, caught early each morning, then sold to and expertly prepared by the seaside restaurants. Thus, le poisson du jour guaranteed a helping of poison. Henceforth, I changed my regular order to mutton and vegetables, which were equally delicious and inexpensive, but presumably less dangerous. The final weeks of the summer melted and blended into the fall term without incident.

At the beginning of the semester, Attila dropped by the office in great distress. He complained in traditional student fashion about his grade. I quickly tuned out the mantra, for I had suffered through the same complaints for decades in various dialects and accents. Nothing new. History records that Aristotle, disappointed in being passed over as *scholarch* of Plato's Academy, had left the groves of Academus for the Lyceum, an ancient school dedicated to Apollo Lyceus. In the case of veteran Attila, I felt certain the injustice actually involved a higher grade than he deserved, not the reverse. At some point a passing remark caught my startled attention: Mrs. Aksoy, a married student of mediocre ability, who had barely earned a B, reported to her classmates that she had received an A in the course. Impossible.

After checking with the registrar, the mystery was solved. Dr. Bugra, who did not know an allomorph from the passive voice, had taken it upon herself to lower one student's grade and raise another's. Having taught in third-world diploma mills for over ten years, I had become inured to the usual incidents of incompetence and corruption. However, that particular outrage set a precedent for pure gall. I determined that the brazen exercise of assumed administrative prerogative had to be addressed.

I immediately wrote Dr. Solak, Vice-Rector, a man of reason with a professional bearing. In my hand-delivered letter, I cited chapter and verse to evident good effect. Sitting magisterially behind a modest desk, he scanned the document. "I'll look into it," he said quietly, giving me the impression that the administrative slippage had occurred in the past. That evening Gul called me at home. "I intend to refute your letter point by point, or I will get all the blame," she added petulantly. Finally, the matter was resolved, at least technically, though I felt far from vindicated. My relationship with the Chair entered a new phase: the night of the long knives. However, owing to Professor Bugra's unsavory reputation as a person unfamiliar with the truth, several colleagues I had never met gratuitously voiced their support.

Weeks later, Mehmet Asani, Dean of Students and Faculty at FU, arrived on campus. He had served as Gul's dissertation advisor in the recent past. In the Orient, the graduate school program was unique in that the advisor ordinarily assumed certain prerogatives well beyond one's ordinary expectations, at least in Western practice. Thus, the usual responsibilities such as research suggestions, editorial comments on each individual chapter, and general encouragement during the long, arduous project were, so to speak, placed on a remote burner—often for the good and sufficient reason that the high-ranking academics, like my Chair at Födz, were total frauds. However, the typical advisor-graduate student relationship was nothing if not complex and interesting.

Thus, the female degree candidate typically served as babysitter, housekeeper, chauffer, and waitress/hostess at family occasions such as weddings, funerals, birthdays, and circumcisions. In keeping with the extra curricular activities, refusal or a lax performance might have resulted in the unkindest cut of all: "no degree." Of course, if all else failed, a young woman desperate for a doctorate might resort to desperate measures. That is, a nubile graduate student could always rely on the ace in the hole, and according to rumor complemented by circumstantial evidence, Dr. Bugra had played that card. Nor had she abandoned the practice at present. She had been observed, according to credible witnesses, leaving the President's office, flushed and in disarray.

Soon after Dr. Asani's triumphal campus appearance, he invited me for a sitdown in his office, across the hall from my modest quarters. When it came to defining his territory and the power that, he assumed, would go with his position at Födz U., Mehmet wasted no time. Within the week, his door in effect read "Behold the Man" in bold letters:

Professor, Dr., hab., Mehmet Asani, AB, MA, PhD.
Dean of Students and Faculty

Consequently, I referred to him in biblical terms as "The Dean of Many Titles."

Our initial conversation included matters of substance. Specifically, he was familiar with the national epic, *Dede Korkut,* and had noticed obvious parallels with *The Odyssey* concerning Polyphemus, the cannibalistic Cyclops. On my part, I contributed the fact that most translations in English read, "We do not fear the Olympians, for we are stronger," in accord with modern notions of status and power. Yet the original was slightly different: "We do not fear the Olympians, because we are *older*." Even more precise: "We do not fear the Olympians, *for we precede them*." The Dean of Many Titles looked pensive, a moment of bonding. However, on referring to various other standard works of literature and criticism, I concluded that our Födz dignitary lacked intellectual substance, an example of Nietzsche's "will to ignorance."

I changed the subject to the deplorable state of the university library. He said that, if I bought suitable texts during my upcoming trip to London, the Department would reimburse my expenditure. Upon departing we shook hands for the first and final time. It occurred to me that the Dean of Faculty had made no mention of my course assignments, much less my qualifications to teach them. Nor did the Dean of Students comment on the overall quality or ethos of our young scholars, who had been largely recruited from the mainland but from other countries as well. Having been burned at Bilkent University, my own concerns about my enforcement of the rules versus departmental policy regarding academic dishonesty remained paramount.

The problem, of course, was commonplace. Indeed, cheating is universal and absolute. As I have observed on other occasions, the methods varied, ranging from crib notes to wandering eyes, from whispered answers to uttering foreign phrases unknown to the instructor. Proxy scholars took exams using phony identity cards, and ghost writers conducted research and composed scholarly papers for pay or even as a token of friendship. Plagiarism had become an American enterprise; at Ohio State University, for example, brochures offering essays on any subject guaranteeing a specific letter grade, for a price, appeared on hall bulletin boards. On their own, students might copy passages/articles verbatim. Variables such as gender, age, religion, mother tongue, and/or nationality had no bearing on the practice: Christians of all denominations; Muslims, Sunni and Shia alike; and Buddhists, Mahayana or Theravāda, have all been known to cut corners.

Nor was deception a recent phenomenon. Satan deceived the mother of mankind; Delilah betrayed Samson; Jacob robbed brother Esau of his birthright; Mary persuaded her cuckold husband that although pregnant, she remained a virgin. Renaissance artisans charged the church authorities for rubies ground into powder used in stained glass windows, though subsequent chemical analyses proved no such precious gems had ever been present. I could go on. . .

Consequently, no one should be surprised that young scholars, competitive and desperate for grades, honors, and degrees, will often resort to the well-known devices—and regularly contrive new techniques to gain advantage. At Födz U., the battle lines were clearly drawn after the summer-school grading scandal, in which the Chair clearly lost face, though Mrs. Aksoy clearly gained an unearned grade.

Determined to have the last word, although we were not on speaking terms, Professor Bugra assigned me an undergraduate course which was in no way linked to my seminar background, teaching experience, or intellectual interest. The text, which I have suppressed, dealt with business matters, which were not exactly legitimate academic concerns—barring of course the hegemony of capitalism and the immutable fact of modern life: the primary importance of a good job. The students, numbering at least seventy men and women, were expected to learn the following: "LASER" decoded means "Light Amplification by the Stimulated Emission of Radiation"; the efficacy of R&R projects; cooperate hierarchies; and various other vacuous acronyms and corporate gimmicks designed to enhance profits, which were produced in Western culture like rare diseases.

Since discussing trivia proved virtually impossible, I gave regular quizzes to ensure progress. Nevertheless, the students produced remarkably similar answers down to factual errors and spelling mistakes. The midterm loomed, and I decided, regardless of time and plain drudgery, to type out four copies of the same test with several statements rearranged, asking the taker to choose one or more correct answers, commonly known as "multiple guess"—an onerous duty, but the tactic worked far beyond expectations.

When my students, after a few minutes, realized they'd been outwitted, their reaction was swift and loud. Although no actual destruction of property occurred, the mob behavior might fairly be described as a controlled riot. I assumed my best poker face and waited. As Estragon stated succinctly in *Waiting for Godot*, "Nothing to be done."

When the racket approached 120 decibels, the threshold of pain, the Vice-Rector appeared without bothering to knock. He sized up the situation quickly and said, "Cliff, the matter is out of control. We must cancel the exam." I gave him a studied look. "Up to you. Not my decision." He told the students to remain in their seats and returned a few minutes later with Gul, who was looking pale and nervous. She told the students to line up as she wrote critical information on a legal pad. I assume she was arranging a retake. As for me, the matter never came to my attention. I walked casually into the hallway, grinning like a raccoon. Time for a snack and a well-earned cup of coffee, Turkish style.

At term's end, Dr. Solak invited me to lunch after attending a post circumcision party on the roof of the main building. Erol, Chief of Faculty Maintenance, who proved more than helpful and friendly, had invited me (the only Westerner) to attend the celebration; his preadolescent son had come of age. The ceremony proved a model of simplicity, with the young "man" sitting in state, his bare lap covered modestly by a blanket, smiling painfully. Each well wisher passed, uttered congratulations in one language or another (I chose *mabrouk*, which was Arabic), and placed a Sterling note amounting to a couple of dollars in his open hand.

My social obligation having met everyone's approval, the Vice-Rector said, "Cliff, I know a restaurant in Lefkosia which serves excellent

Iskender kebab. Will you join me?" We arrived soon after the regular lunch crowd and sat near the window, with a clear view of the guard tower separating the two island nations. Half way through the Greek salad, liberally studded with black olives and sprinkled with genuine extra-virgin olive oil, I made my case in plain English, not omitting a few street-corner phrases, and concluded by stating, "Dr. Bugra is an insufferable, incompetent bitch with zero redeeming qualities. She also has many negative traits."

The Rector's fork clicked against the plate. "Cliff," he replied half angry, half pleading, "don't make me choose!" I glanced out the window at the changing of the guard. "Well, I know something about choice, having taught *Being & Nothingness* for over ten years." He missed the allusion, but understood my point. "Okay," he said by way of a belated apology for the exam fiasco, which he had witnessed first-hand, "how would you like a graduate seminar in a course of your choosing?" I held my straight look and said, "No interference from Ms. Rosebud." He nearly smiled. "You have my word, which I hope is good," he replied, turning to the melted-butter waiter and pointing to my plate of mutton. *Kill him with kindness—and cholesterol*, I mused inwardly.

The course on modernism proved an unmitigated disaster. Before examining *The Dubliners*, the first text under consideration, I defined basic terms: plot, structure, foreshadowing, symbol, irony, paradox, image, epiphany, and so on. Halfway through my monologue on "Araby," I realized that most of the scholars had problems reading the story on the literal level. At midterm, I assigned an outside paper with a list of suggested topics: setting and character, politics and religion, psychology and society. "Choose two elements in any story and indicate a conflict, tension, influence—any thesis that requires analysis and/or interpretation. Suggest your own topic; if it seems reasonable I will offer advice, a strategy, ideas. Show me your draft, and I will edit the essay for you." Nothing!

The night before the paper was due, I received a phone call. "Professor Hallam, we want an extension." I refused. "But no one in the class has written a paper." I resented the conspiracy, but withheld judgment. "We will address this matter tomorrow in class," I said and hung up. As a scarred veteran of political infighting, I tended to avoid appeasement, which never satisfied bullies; first it's the Czech Republic, then it's Poland. Yet draconian measures were rarely advised. I held out the possibility of persuasion, though, as Heidegger stated, "the dreadful had already occurred."

The next day at the appointed hour, one paper appeared on my desk. Attila, the only man in the course, had produced a handwritten document running to a thousand words, as required. I admonished the slackers for irresponsible behavior, the contrived late-hour announcement, and I reset the assignment. No one would earn a grade above a B-, which was barely passing. The women groaned; Attila objected strongly. Sensing tactical advantage, he refused to budge. After all, he had fulfilled the assignment and deserved a reward, at least an A-. I dismissed the class, and the women filed out. Atilla remained to haggle like a self-righteous customer in the *souq*. At some point I told him that I would read his essay in light of his unique position, but made no promises. Predictably, the paper did not meet college-level standards. The expression verged on stream of consciousness without the aesthetic compensations. A few passages were clearly plagiarized or ghost-written.

Attila appeared at my office threshold before class the next morning demanding a verdict, which I delivered: expulsion from the Modernism Seminar. He turned and headed straight for his defender, Dr. Bugra, to plead his case. Surely, in his view, the only student to submit his assignment on time had been wronged. Meanwhile, I wrote the Vice-Rector in order to cover myself. Upon checking my mail the next day, I received a reply—but not from the Chair, who had evidently decided during an earlier confrontation over grade-changing to keep her own counsel. In this one instance, she chose the course of wisdom. Certainly, I was in no mood for another exercise in foolishness, falsehoods, and stupidity. And although I harbored a laundry list of complaints concerning her unprofessional conduct, including the calumny that a graduate student had sold exams on the streets of

Lefkosia, I preferred to let matters rest for the moment. Let us not, as Dr. Kinbote observed, "pursue the tabulation of nonsense."

I quickly read the short note. "Mr. Hallam: You are not to harass, browbeat, humiliate, or downgrade any student enrolled at Födz University. Signed, Dr. hab. Mehmet Asani, Dean of Faculty and Students."

I had learned, after some unfortunate consequences in my youth, to control a volatile temper. Consequently, when provoked I typically waited until the appropriate occasion to respond in civil fashion. Not this time. Within a few minutes, I found the Dean in an empty classroom, tutoring an unusually backward student in basic English. Inside, I stood a few feet from the door and beckoned him to come closer. As he approached, I considered that the old man, suffering from diabetes, would not likely survive a focused punch. Moreover, the Near East was not a model of Platonic justice. Thus, if I had assaulted the Dean under any circumstances, I would have faced serious consequences. "Look," I said sharply, "this memo is out of line. Watch yourself." I then turned and left before he could reply. Completely unsatisfied with the faux confrontation, I later typed a note: "To the Dean of Many Titles: You know nothing of the matter." I scribbled my initials below the statement and taped the document to the office door beneath the string of letters.

For approximately a week, no word. Then during class break, I found a terse note in my mailbox instructing me to meet with another Vice-Rector, a man unknown to me. Seething, I marched to the administration building up the hill and confronted a receptionist with the document. "Who's this?" I demanded. At that moment, an elderly gentlemen with a hearing aid called from a nearby hallway entrance. "Doctor Hallam? Would you kindly follow me, please?" With the Vice-Rector leading the way, I negotiated a labyrinth of hallways with no staff members in evidence, a Kafkan dream-like route deeper into the building's interior.

Finally, Dr. Cevdet paused at a doorway and invited me to enter a small office with no furniture, save a cluttered desk and a comfortable chair. "Have a seat, sir," he said, motioning. Suddenly, a high-pitched screech broke the silence. The Vice-Rector carefully adjusted the hearing apparatus and cleared his throat. "I know he can be difficult," he said softly. I waited several seconds. "Whom do you mean?" I replied. Dr. Cevdet looked slightly confused; he glanced at his desk, then at me. "Well, the Dean," he said just barely audible. "Tell my students," I said in measured tones, "another time, another place." I then reached for my briefcase, stood up, and headed out. As I made my way to the main office, I heard a plaintive voice, like Brandon DeWilde calling after Alan Ladd in *Shane*: "Doctor Hallam, Doctor Hallam. Come back." Like the lone gunslinger with no past and a single name, I did not answer—nor did I return.

I called a cab from my office, and reaching the sole travel agency in Lefkosia in a matter of minutes, I made arrangements for a flight to Istanbul early the next morning. All proceeded according to plan. I reached the airport at dawn and boarded the plane without bureaucratic hassle or interference from the authorities. "These cretins are capable of anything," I muttered, but no one guessed I had taken French leave, as I later discovered after returning to the States.

The milk run to Istanbul was uneventful, but I faced a long journey ahead. The small hotel in the old quarter was playing host to a convention, so no rooms were available without a reservation. The manager remembered me, however, as a regular guest when in town and rented me a tiny room on the top floor. I then took the airport shuttle to confirm my ticket. The desk clerk said that I had to return the next morning at least an hour before departure to clear a one-way passage with the supervisor. She asked for a $20 deposit in US currency, which promptly fell between the large booths and could not be retrieved.

The following day, the supervisor took a cursory glance at my $835 ticket and pronounced it invalid, so I bought another with my credit card. While waiting in line, a security officer demanded to see my passport. Flipping expertly through the pages, she stopped, stared, and frowned. "Why you go to Arabic countries?" she asked. "I spent time in the Middle East and decided to visit Damascus. Bought some tablecloths and souvenirs for friends and family." She continued examining various exotic stamps. "I will take this to the commander. Don't think you will make this flight." A few minutes later, she handed me the passport without further comment.

Landing in Frankfurt, I bought sausage encased in thick plastic. After crossing the Atlantic, unable to sleep, I landed in New York, where the customs official asked to see the *wurst*, which I had noted on my entry card, and promptly confiscated the link. He said shortly, "Could be infected with rinderpest," which in fact had been virtually eliminated worldwide. Upon opening my checked luggage at home, I discovered that a baggage handler had admired my custom folder, worth several hundred dollars, and had appropriated my knife.

It was 1993, and although safe at home, I was in a bind: fifty-four years old, no job, no prospects, no place to live, and definitely no let-ters of recommendation from Födz University. Ruefully, I recalled the subtitle of T.E. Lawrence's masterpiece of failure and defeat, *Seven Pillars of Wisdom: A Triumph*. Taking refuge in radical irony, I considered my next career move: an application to Łódz University in Poland. I considered the country's well-earned reputation for anti-Semitism, but falsely assumed that, like American slavery, the good citizens had consigned the shameful record of human abuse to the past.

By the mid-90s, while living in a Snopes trailer in southern Indiana, America seemed like a temporary dwelling, a familiar place to gather myself and prepare for the next exotic adventure, as expressed by the Milton persona, "To morrow to fresh Woods, and Pastures new."

VI.

Poland Unbound[1]

It gathers and its scatters; it comes and it goes.

—Heraclitus

Łödz is Poland's third-largest city, located about 135 kilometers from Warsaw, the capital. Oddly enough, "Łödz" is pronounced "woodj" and means "boat," though the urban center remains landlocked. During the Russian occupation, a robust economy had depended on textile manufacture—at a price. The dyes had polluted rivers, ground, and air and virtually annihilated wildlife, except for pigeons, while reducing life expectancy.

In 1994, when I taught American literature and theory at the university in Łödz, major factories had been shut, and the environment sympathetically lacked color. The sky, buildings, and scant vegetation reflected shades of metallic grey. The older generation, which had endured decades of political repression first by Nazis, then by Communists, had acquired ashen complexions, complementing the environment.

The pall served as a legacy imposed by the Russian dictatorship, which effectively had devastated the entire country. An implicit question, then, demanded a measured response: I was eager to learn how the Polish citizens were appreciating and coping with their newfound freedom and responsibility.

The social pattern evolved a binary grouping—the older versus the younger. Men, ranging from young adults to pensioners, reeled about the streets, clutching bottles of cheap vodka or wine. In winter, drunks lay frozen on the sidewalks, unattended by pedestrians, who ignored the casualties and continued on their way. In contrast to the victims

[1] December 2014 *Curitiba in English*, edit. Michael Rubin.

were the children who had come of age after the Soviet plague had withdrawn, and most, like my advanced university students, remained aloof from their elders—poles apart, in a manner of speaking.

My graduate students, like their European/American counterparts, demonstrated curiosity and ambition, driven not by alcohol, but by the conviction that most anything was possible through personal effort in an open society. The late twentieth-century generation, largely unaffected by Stalinist communism, eagerly embraced the wonders of capitalist opportunity grounded in political freedom. Once directed toward tangible goals, virtually impossible under the Soviet system, no sacrifice in time or amount of tedious work mattered.

The first items upon arriving in Poland: unpack, store my clothes, arrange books, and settle in my apartment. Since WWII, entire families, including divorced couples, had shared one cramped apartment, for which people had sold out their dignity under the Russian occupation. By contrast, I was provided by the university—rent free—a furnished five-room flat. My living quarters were comfortable, but no threat to an American condo or high-end suite. Upon entering my shabby apartment, Polish guests invariably asked, "Cliff, do you live here alone?" I often rehearsed a favorite gag. Visitor: "Where's the toilet?" Host: "You're in it." My Polish friends were nonplussed by the punch line. For although I resided in a Soviet-style ghetto (Bałuti, in fact, was the Jewish quarter during the War) with drab buildings arranged like dominoes, my modest apartment inspired wonder and envy. As a product of runaway free enterprise rife with corruption, fraud, endless scams, invasive advertising, and pressure to succeed, I would sometimes reply to an ambitious enthusiast bent on making it big: "Are you sure this is what you want?"

Exceptions of course did not prove the rule—quite the opposite—but anomalies tested the paradigm. One of my outstanding students was a case in point. Like most Łödz residents, he lived with his parents, siblings, and grandmother in a cramped apartment. His parents slept behind closed doors, while the rest of the residents had to shift for themselves. The senior family member claimed the sofa, while two brothers dozed on a futon. My young charge slept fitfully on an over-stuffed chair with a broken back to accommodate his slender six-foot frame. He studied at the miniscule university library, where the dimly lit reading room provided warmth with a measure of peace and quiet.

Yet my hopeful friend somehow had earned a master's degree and later a doctorate, despite his unproductive scholarship time spent traveling with his business partner to nearby Germany twice a week. During a conversation over tea and *paczki* (Polish donuts), I made mention of his sleep patterns, wondering where he found the time for rest. "What's that?" he enquired half-seriously.

Generalizations about people of any description seldom held; thus, the American preconception regarding Polish lack of intelligence or laziness was immediately put to the test. I can verify the fact that my students were exceptionally bright and hard working. Additionally, my fellow university professors proved among the best-prepared scholars I have known in my long and varied career. One and all of my colleagues demonstrated unusual aptitude and skill in pursuit of their studies, despite that fact that the Russian occupiers required a pass to leave the city, which afforded little opportunity for research. My Polish friends and associates often described bureaucratic night-mares, yet they somehow endured. Nevertheless, my colleagues' scholarship was impressive. For example, Professor Kristoff Andrze-jczak completed his habilitation manuscript, a study of the post WWII *Künstlerroman*. He produced a work of deep and specialized scholar-ship, which was later published in several editions. Moreover, I attended a number of high-powered conferences during my stay in Poland and profited a great deal from the presentations / discussions.

Łödz University hired Dr. Matthew Gibson and myself to direct sem-inars in British and American literature, respectively. Unlike my col-league, I am literally dumbfounded when visiting non-English speaking countries. Dr. Gibson, an accomplished polyglot, speaks the major European languages, plus Polish, Russian, and Bulgarian. Con-sequently, in addition to Matthew's companionship, I appreciated his translating skills during our frequent junkets to Warsaw, Krakow, Italy, and Vienna during our Łödz tenure. The Dean encouraged the travels in order to broaden our experience and make use of well-stocked libraries outside the country.

One afternoon, while sampling Polish vodka at a local bistro with Matthew, I said half-jokingly that the purpose of existence was to fool around and have fun. "So I've noticed," he replied drily. Overseas friendships grounded in such nuanced experiences can last a lifetime and, although separated by oceans and continents, we still keep in touch.

Teaching assignments in remote countries tend to attract exceptional individuals of both extremes. At lunch with the Chair, who had studied at Yale and was thus familiar with "Yankee" individualists, I attempted to explain a fellow American, whose eccentric behavior was attracting unfavorable attention. I tactfully pointed out that the instructor, Richard Lecklus, did appear a bit odd. The Chair promptly replied, "And so do you, Cliff. Otherwise you wouldn't be here." Touché.

Like Ivan Denisovich in the Solzhenitsyn novella, I learned the ropes as a traveling scholar. While living and working in remote countries, a smooth adjustment to a new life remained crucial for personal, social, and political reasons. As a denizen of Łödz, however, I could not ignore the rampant anti-Semitism. Public buildings, trolley shelters, and even the Jewish graveyard enclosures were vandalized with graffiti: a gallows, star of David in the noose, "raus Juden" in German, and the English phrase "Hitler was right." During an election campaign, a popular magazine published the candidates' photos with the caption "Which one is the Jew?"

Significantly, on April 30, 1995 (the fiftieth anniversary of Hitler's death), neo-Nazis, under the cover of night, plastered posters depicting a thug with a sledgehammer striking the Star of David under the heading "Smash Judaism." The posters covered every available façade, wall, and utility pole. The following day, I presented one such poster to the Provost of the university, who mumbled that the soccer club might have been responsible. He added only that the anti-Semitic propaganda would be promptly removed. It wasn't. During class I pointed out to the students that a predominantly Christian country that had produced a pope (later beatified) bore the responsibility for racist dogma. No one argued the point, but few actively supported my position. I left Poland at the end of the semester.

In retrospect, my stay in Łödz provoked contradictory feelings ranging from admiration to disappointment, from aesthetic fulfillment to utter disgust. Today, government functionaries in Poland no longer insist on legal double binds. The hotels, restaurants, and shops on *ulica Piotrkowska* are blossoming; their once-barren show windows are bursting with a profusion of high-quality goods. World-class scholarship has asserted itself in conferences, articles, books, and translations. Free of occupation, the *Polska* of Copernicus, who revolutionized astronomy; Chopin, whose musical compositions enthralled millions worldwide; Madame Skłodowska Curie, who was awarded the Nobel Prize in physics; and Kosciuszko, the patriotic general who secured West Point in 1778; has come into its own.

However, there is also a dark side to Poland; indeed, the shadow of its past and continued present should not be ignored or forgotten. Yet, the post-Berlin Wall generation today in Poland has joined the community of democracies, and the nascent society, with its legacy of scientists, musicians, artists, writers, and intellectuals, is thriving. Moreover, as a NATO member, the Central European country effectively protects the infamous Polish Corridor, which provoked conflicts, invasions, and decades of totalitarian rule. On balance, then, Poland is poised to evolve constructively, address past grievances, and sustain an unprecedented era under the rule of law.

VII.

Grime and Drunkenness

And for a season after
Could not believe but that I was in hell... — Shakespeare

Stark against the slate-grey sky, the multi-colored onion domes of St. Basil's cathedral, vibrant against a dull background, met my expectations, along with a sense of *déjà vu*. As a child of the Cold War, the Red Square landmark served as metonymy, emblematic of Soviet power and threat. By the 1950s, however, with the balance of terror at its height, the Stalinist police state had rotted from within—although the actual crash heard round the world did not occur until the fabled Berlin Wall, attacked ironically with sledge hammers, if not sickles, was breached in 1989. German citizens about to be liberated from both sides of the wall literally danced along the narrow top of the formidable barrier while being hosed down by East Berlin security personnel. The rest is history...

Arriving in Moscow on the overnight train from Minsk, I hailed a cab at the depot and managed in my garbled Russian to state my destination as had been written in English by Ilya Denisovich Stukov, Vice Provost and Department Head at Minsk State Linguistic University, where I was to teach undergraduate literature courses, graduate seminars, and history of ideas as a Fulbright scholar, 1998–99.

As a long-time faculty member, I knew the Moscow colloquium held special significance for both literary and political reasons: top authors/scholars from the United States regularly attended the annual convention, and a meeting of the minds, like musical and sports events, proved to presumed antagonists that the hated capitalists and communists, respectively, offered no imminent threat. Participants soon came to realize that after a firm handshake or powerful bear hug, all humans strove for satisfaction and fulfillment in a similar manner. Thus, each friendly, sincere exchange meant another chink in the great wall that literally and metaphorically separated East from West.

Yet a decade after the collapse of the Soviet Empire, the Moscow University Literary Conference, from my first impression of the academic venue, no longer met eager anticipations, nor figured as an especially unique opportunity to exchange ideas, mutual invitations, and personal addresses. The large hall, magnificent in its time, foretold the quality of the learned papers and esteemed lecturers: overall, a bit shabby and second rate. Just inside the door, wide stairways were drafty in the under-heated building, and the promise of grandeur was not kept. Rat holes punctuated the peeling wainscot, and in-house pigeons circled the atrium, minus the conventional glass roof, searching for food scraps left by careless visitors.

The spacious lecture room, lined with old books and faded photographs of *apparatchiks* who had served the State, as opposed to the literary dialectic, seemed unwelcoming, compounded by a musty smell combined with cheap tobacco smoke. Out of a nineteenth-century Russian novel, a huge silver *samovar* squatted on an oval table, while a dozen tea glasses, none-too-clean, were lined in a row. A chipped bowl of yellowish sugar lumps the size of hickory nuts and topped with antique tongs completed the tableau. Invited quests— including graduate students, faculty members, scholars of various disciplines, and political minders—mingled about the room, conversing in low tones.

Predictably, Dr. Ivan Vladimir Malarsky served as the conference director, scowling at lesser mortals under thick eyebrows like grey caterpillars. He sat in a wide executive chair, wearing a rumpled yellow raincoat festooned with black buttons—a private detective gone to seed. By his side, he kept a worn, leather briefcase crammed with texts, notebooks, and papers. He projected an image of constant industry. Trusted by the Politboro, Professor Malarsky read widely in Western texts (both officially accepted and proscribed), translated scores of canonical titles in all genres, and published his thoughts at will. Within the hermetic political system, he was virtually impossible to challenge; if discretion was the better part of valor, those who had decided on a literary career within the Soviet Union even after its breakup habitually kissed the ring.

Upon entering the conference room, my Minsk colleague Ilya greeted me, and we exchanged phatic ping-pong: "How was your trip?"; "Comfortable in the sleeping car?"; "Looking forward to your paper." Ilya, Dr. Malarsky's prize student, by then an established academic in his own right, was accorded special privileges, such as introducing visiting scholars. Dr. Stukov then ushered me to the Great Man sprawled regally in the great Chair: "Professor Malarsky, I have brought our American literature professor, as promised." Remaining seated, Ivan extended a beefy hand and said, "We will cooperate." Having already spent some twenty years in foreign countries, I accepted such *non-sequiturs* as the norm. Portfolio presented and grudgingly accepted, I joined the faculty members and graduate students for hot, sweet tea.

The formal introduction, like the conference itself, could be described as a non-event. In fact, the famous Russian scholar and I had already met at the American Literature Conference in Minsk. Working in Poland at the time, I had learned of the colloquium a day or two before the affair began. My Chair, at the behest of the US State Department representative, had invited me to read a paper in Belarus so that at least one native speaker should have attended the taxpayer-sponsored function.

After spending the night off Independence Square in a drab hotel noted for providing Lee Harvey Oswald a room shortly after he had defected to the Soviet Union, I took the nearby subway well before 8:00 a.m. as a hedge against losing my way in a strange city, in which English was rarely spoken away from the several universities. The subway stopped near Minsk State, which was announced over a speaker. The Russian "universidad" sounded like English with a heavy accent. Crossing Victory Square, with its obelisk topped by the communist insignia and its eternal flame, I entered the building with anticipation, as I had always admired Russian literary masterpieces and scholarship.

The conference room, already crowded with literary scholars from exotic locations like Kiev, Petersburg, and Tobolsk (Siberia), featured a long table covered with open-faced sandwiches and soft drinks for the invited lecturers. Dr. Stukov, whom I knew from a Kosiński conference in Poland, served as my front man. Everyone was gracious, cordial, even rather thrilled to meet a genuine American professor. Although I did not affect a tweed sports jacket with leather elbow patches and a briar pipe, my cowhide briefcase no doubt satisfied everyone's idea of a literature professor from the States.

I noticed a large, balding comrade, steely eyed, striding across the hall. It was Dr. Ivan Vladimir Malarsky. Professor Stukov took us each by the arm, beaming. Upon the introduction, Malarsky immediately established his credentials as the alpha male by handing me his pretentious business card printed in both Latin and Cyrillic characters while asking for mine, which I failed to produce. He grunted in a disapproving manner, clearly suggesting that the vacuous exchange indicated status and competence in the field.

Throughout the weeklong gala event, Ivan never failed to provide an impromptu speech at each session, well larded with authoritative opinions in the guise of *ex cathedra* pronouncements. If the pope was infallible in matters of faith and morals, then Malarsky claimed similar authority in literary criticism, though he was clearly deficient in matters of theory. In one droning commentary, he extolled the merits of Robert Stone's virtually unreadable *Outerbridge Reach*, while casually dismissing the author's earlier work, including *A Flag for Sunrise*, *Dog Soldiers*, and *Children of Light*, as novels of little consequence. He then concluded his rambling talk with a directive: "And so to work."

In the days ahead, I soon realized (and not for the first time) that Clio, the muse of history, was an ironist. While reading my paper on

Pale Fire, I made reference to *ostranenie*, a key Russian formalist term translated as "defamiliarization," which, like "trope," takes many forms. At that moment I noticed several seated colleagues looking up and indicating unusual interest in my presentation. Later, during the break, two or three Russian speakers, all women, enquired about the term, which they understood etymologically to mean "placing an object in an unfamiliar context," like floating an orange in a tar pool, thus defamiliarizing the item. The early twentieth-century Russian formalists had borrowed the term to mean "the unique qualities of literary texts," as opposed to strictly informative ones—not the function of imagery, so important to Anglo-American formalists, but to foreground, for example, "the stoniness of stone."

Having read Victor Erlich's standard work on the movement and its features, I recalled the fact that Stalin had decreed, arbitrarily, that the revolutionary critical method should be outlawed as counterrevolutionary—a prime example of Soviet paralogy. A purge followed: outstanding scholars had faced censure, exile, even execution; and major texts had disappeared from the massive Lenin library, as well as from lesser book hoards throughout the empire. A decade later, despite loosening censorship and the Kremlin's wide acceptance by the West, little money had been spared for scholarship, so *de facto* censorship remained.

My Russian counterparts by way of rumor and references in popular magazines/journals had eventually learned of Russian formalism *per se*, but none had read deeply in theory, since travel and access remained restricted in the brave new world following the Russian Empire *de casibus* of 1991. Delighted at an opportunity to explain the major tenets, along with illustration, I too set to work, as Malarsky had directed. For an example of parallelism, I borrowed J.Y. Douglas' brilliant insight into a passage of *Mrs. Dalloway* in which Peter Walsh, while thinking of Clarissa, hears an ambulance siren screaming down Tottenham Court Road in answer to Septimus Smith's suicide. Hours later Clarissa, Smith's literary double, whom she never met, learns of the WWI veteran's death at her party.

For baring the device, a postmodern novel provides this striking simile: "if you take a breath and feel like a broken window. . ." Moreover, I explained the difference between *syuzhet*, the artistic arrangement of the incidents, as opposed to the *fabula*, the chronology of events. The private tutorial lasted well into the afternoon, and some of the presenters were deprived of a full audience. So it came to pass that an American, familiar with Schklovsky, Medvedev, Bakhtin, and Jakobsen in translation, plus commentaries by Frederic Jameson, Terry Eagleton, and the above-mentioned Victor Erlich, revealed the mysteries of Russian formalism to those best able to understand the original texts. As Lacan observed, "The letter is always delivered."

On the second day of the conference, Ilya and I took a tram to a rundown hotel in order to book rooms for scholars arriving late from the outer reaches of Siberia. Inside the foyer, a pensioner with bloodshot eyes and suspicious breath guarded the entrance. Although my command of the language barely exceeded greetings, asking directions, or requesting stamps at the Central Post Office, I grasped his hand and uttered polite phrases. He grinned and muttered a response that did not register, but I understood him to mean that I was welcome. The old man then turned to Ilya and engaged in rapid conversation, while often glancing at me in a conspiratorial manner.

Later at the trolley shelter, I asked Ilya to translate: "All my life I have believed that Americans are bad people. Why, he's just like us!" I reflected on the epiphany. Following a series of errors by politicians on both sides of the Iron Curtain, we might have faced each other armed with an M1 and AK-47, respectively, across the barricades. Yet a firm handshake, eye contact , a few words exchanged in his native tongue, and we had bonded forever! Thus, as I have often observed, entrenched racism, bigotry, and xenophobia may melt like snow on a cherry-red pot-bellied stove after brief, authentic contact with the dreaded Other.

At the Moscow conference, meanwhile, Professor Malarsky, who played the university commissar to perfection, opened the proceedings two hours late with a bravura performance, not overlooking his own considerable contributions to Soviet letters as professor, author, dissertation director, and translator without peer. Tovarich Ivan then returned to his seat and announced briefly the first presenter, Yuri Datsik: a young graduate student who had attended my public lectures on literary theory in Minsk. The bright young man, under Dr. Malarsky's direction, had recently arrived at the dissertation stage. One more hurdle, and he, too, might join the few, the proud, and the arrogant of Russian letters.

Shorn of his great coat, Yuri nevertheless retained a classic Russian cap made of genuine fox fur, complete with its snarling head. Yuri glanced at scattered, handwritten notes as he expounded on Pynchon's early work, without much evidence of a thesis or clear focus. After he concluded his disjointed observations, I ventured a question: "As *Doubtfire* clearly establishes theme and content for later Robert Nye novels, do you consider *Slow Learner* equally important in this regard?" I intended the query as a gift, expecting the young doctoral student to expound at length. Yet I was disappointed. In fact, he had obviously never heard of the text. Malarsky then suggested that he had paid little attention to the masterpiece, *Gravity's Rainbow*, which he evidently had not read, either. With this promising start, it was my turn to expound.

I read a Derridean approach to James Dickey's *Deliverance*. In that instance I broke precedent, since the article could not be described as virginal; in fact, I had read the essay in Poznań, Poland, plus it had already been published. I did not, however, blush inwardly; my postcommunist comrades, despite their degrees, titles, and publications, had often expressed their racist, anti-Semitic views and expected me—as an assumed, bigoted WASP—to concur. Some challengers, according to the code of honor, were simply un-duelable. Grinding my molars, I typically failed to respond to pure nonsense and abruptly changed the topic.

As a case in point, my Minsk translator, a bright young man who had actually lived in the States and spoke warmly of his "second family" in Florida, offered the following exercise in political conspiracy: Monica Lewinsky had deliberately saved her sperm-stained dress in order to provide evidence for the Republican Senators' intent on impeaching President Clinton. The motive? Al Gore, who was Jewish, would assume the office in order to promote the Zionist takeover of first America and later the world. I had replied that Vice President Gore was a Scots-Irish Baptist with no plans for a *coup.* "Morever," I added, "no sensible person believes in conspiracy theories. It's hard enough to get three guys together for lunch." My translator had shrugged and suggested dinner at the Planetta, the sole five-star hotel in Minsk. With no exceptions, I picked up the tab, a matter of several million rubles but less than $2 USD, including tip.

Back in Moscow, I concluded my *Deliverance* paper with a quote from *Civilization and Its Discontents*, where Freud observes that owing to innate aggression, "As a result [of their aggressiveness], their neighbor. . .tempts them. . .to exploit his capacity for work without compensation, to use him sexually without his consent, to seize his possessions, to humiliate him, to cause him pain, to torture and to kill him." For long seconds, silence. No questions, no applause, no eye contact. I expressed my thanks and replaced the essay in my briefcase. *"Not a great success,"* I reflected, vacating the podium.

Finally, Dr. Malarsky, who had attended my analysis of *Pale Fire* in Minsk two years prior, offered a rare, if lame, compliment. "I see that you have not lost your enthusiasm for the twentieth-century novel." He then added, "Why didn't you include something about Dickey's poetry?" After such question, what reply? For once, I was at a loss for words. Throughout my career, I had encouraged students to expose themselves, if necessary, by simple-minded enquiries. "There is no such thing as a stupid question," I had insisted. But then, after decades of teaching/lecturing in America and abroad, I found I had been dead wrong. Malarsky's had been, by any definition, a stupid question.

During the hiatus, although many presenters were patiently waiting in the wings, someone called out the names of the American participants.

"Could you all come to the tea table, please?" Once assembled, my four East-coast colleagues and I were shaken down, Soviet style. Exchanging uneasy glances, we listened to the surprise announcement: In appreciation for Moscow University privileges (which were not much in evidence) foreign scholars were required to join a learned society, in which inclusion meant an opportunity to read the conference papers, which might well be published (actually, no proceedings reached the university press), and each new member would receive a monthly newsletter— which in fact, like the above promised benefits, did not exist. The fee: $100 USD. An interesting, round number, certainly, and an opportunity for our Russian colleagues to examine several images of Ben Franklin, who had discovered the source of electricity during the reign of the tsars.

By late afternoon, with frequent tea breaks, the audience had grown restless. The quality of scholarship, for the most part mediocre, functioned as a soporific. During the drone of still another explication of *Martin Eden*, a dreary novel by Jack London, whose Socialist views inspired Marxist analysis *ad nauseam*, some auditors drifted off, no doubt dreaming of a Workers' Paradise that had never come to be. Ironically, despite the emphasis on communist brotherhood as an earned ideal, London's racist views (e.g., "yellow peril" to describe Chinese immigrants) were overlooked by many Soviet literary critics. As respite for rationalizing Eden's suicide by way of the dialectic, a Minsk professor who had survived the siege of Leningrad extolled the virtues of *Our Town*.

I listened carefully for a well-reasoned, substantial argument, but failed to identify one. After the peroration, I raised my hand. "Is this soft-boiled vision of New England Americana not an impressionistic description of a time and place that never existed?" I then suggested that we were lulled into a world informed by false consciousness belying the suffering of the proletariat. Professor Galena literally stuttered in a feeble attempt to reply. Dr. Malarsky, conferring with a Kiev colleague, broke off the conversation and rose majestically to his feet. "Let me say a few words," he intoned. "Years ago I translated much of Wilder's work, including *Our Town*. In my view, the play emphasizes the fraternal order of society: a system that, in America at least, shows a possible future social organization, something within its grasp and worth the struggle."

He then formally concluded the session, and people shuffled into the hall. Ilya quickly approached and whispered an invitation to a private gathering, to better savor the proceedings informally. I, along with about a dozen high-ranking Russian scholars, waited until the conference room had cleared before descending a narrow stairway to the dining hall located below street level. A heavyset professor from Siberia fell into stride and asked me, without preamble, to define "deconstruction." I hesitated and replied, "More than one definition, but I can offer some characteristic features of the philosophy, ranging from the inherent instability of the text, any text, to the often ironizing function of tropes, as DeMan demonstrates in his analysis of the inside/outside passage from Proust." After a short silence she said, "We will talk about this again. Thank you so much."

Inside the large, well-appointed room, I found myself seated two chairs away from the redoubtable Malarsky, who once again set the tone with a long-winded speech about the successful conference (*"With several days to go,"* I observed silently), sparing himself no credit for the auspicious beginning. Ilya, sitting across from me, made eye contact. "You're next," he lip-synched. *"Me?"* I replied silently pointing to my chest. He nodded emphatically. Within less than a minute, I was on my feet in my orational mode, with Ilya simultaneously translating for the few non-English speakers.

I focused on Dostoyevsky's famous passage in *The Brothers Karamazov*: without religious values and sanctions, "everything is permitted." I went on to observe that the modern era punctuated by its world wars with carpet-bombing, atrocities, pogroms, and Holocaust proved the observation. However, as the international conference and like occasions suggest, we can conduct ourselves in better fashion. Thank you." I took my seat to a round of applause.

Not to be outdone, Dr. Malarsky without invitation rose and said, "I do not take a pessimistic view of the twentieth century, which is coming to a close. We have witnessed great changes for the better. Material progress, the virtual disappearance of class distinctions in selected instances, great strides in science and technology, space exploration, and advances in modern medicine all point to a better world and a superior system to conduct our social and political affairs. We should not dwell on mishaps, which are historically inevitable, mere residue of the dialectic, but hold fast to our ideals." He cleared his throat. "Give us a moment to provide refreshment."

Waiters in white coats appeared, placing trays of open-faced sandwiches, along with a bottle of excellent vodka, labeled "The Magician," on the long wooden table. Famished, since I had subsisted on tea since arriving in Moscow, I selected the black caviar, salt herring, smoked salmon, and hard-boiled egg delicacies. I rarely drank alcohol beyond one or two shots and never straight vodka, so I searched in vain for familiar brands of soda: Coke, Pepsi, Fanta. . . None. On a separate table, however, I found tea, coffee, and hard cider.

A tall, lean man, fit like an aging athlete, placed his hand on my shoulder, greeting me in guttural Russian and directed me to the buffet. Filling two glasses with vodka, he first downed a herring sandwich and, muttering "*nasdrovye*," swallowed the fiery liquid in three gulps, his prominent Adam's apple bobbing the full length of his muscular throat. I concluded correctly that I owed the honor to a member of the KGB. Handing me the herring *hors d'oeuvre*, followed by a dollop of vodka, he indicated that I should follow the example. I gladly devoured the sandwich, but only sipped the alcohol. By that time I knew the drill: toast follows toast until one of the merry pranksters was literally on the floor. I could see clearly how the session would end.

But not so fast, comrade *Amerikanze*. With little concern for a civil tone, the Russian officer sternly lectured me concerning social obligations in Mother Russia. Although I understood little, I definitely got the idea. "Well, I have to work tomorrow," I said in English. He smirked and replied in his own idiom: "Tovarich, work is not a wolf. It won't run into the woods." Point well taken, but I nevertheless took my leave and joined Ilya for a lively discussion of late Henry James novels. The question at hand: "Does anyone but a specialist or doctoral candidate in late nineteenth-century fiction read them twice?"

Glancing across the room, my potential drinking buddy glared like the wolf in the homely comparison. As I remarked to Ilya, who had said that Dr. Marlarsky could make trouble under the slightest pretext, "Luckily, I am out of his reach." I raised my glass of cider, smirked, and turned to my fellow presenters, who were examining Edith Wharton as a transitional figure in American letters.

My interest in *The Age of Innocence* remaining minimal, I drifted apart from the learned council and, in view of my recent decision to remain sober, reflected on the commonplace observation that the drunkenness of the Danes informed a pattern of corruption imagery in *Hamlet*. So, too, in post-communist states, according to my experience: namely Łódz and Minsk. Over a two-year period (1994–96), while living and working in the notorious Polish corridor, I had personally witnessed fallen men, literally dead-drunk, on the sidewalks. Alcoholism and Soviet communism, like the famous Siamese twins, were joined; however, by the late nineties, many young Poles had turned their attention and considerable energy to constructive projects, such as starting a business or buying a house. Drinking vodka, although not entirely abandoned as a social enterprise, no longer controlled their lives.

In Minsk, I sometimes shopped at the neighborhood "Magazine" (from the Arabic "storehouse") for basic commodities, though not always available, much less appetizing. One well-stocked shelf of cheap vodka, however, had replaced religion as the opiate of the people. I sometimes noticed the customer next in line at the checkout counter had loaded his shopping basket with liquid oblivion and nothing else. Moreover, the underground tunnels at traffic intersections built to protect pedestrians resembled a socialist gauntlet: both sides lined with squatters, bottle in one hand, the other outstretched for small change, mumbling gibberish. In subway stations, obnoxious drunks were regularly frog-marched by police officers wearing camouflage and polished jump boots to a black maria, conveniently parked near the entrance.

Minsk was an old-style police state. Lukashenko, "the last European dictator," brooked no dissent. Political rivals tended to disappear: prison sentences on trumped-up charges, unexplained exile, mysterious death by poisoning. Moreover, he subsidized the production of cheap vodka (75¢ per liter), which functioned as a form of population control via cirrhosis of the liver. Otherwise, the Stalinist regime controlled media, computer communication, and travel permits, which might have taken months to process, if at all.

Since publication of *1984* shortly after WWII, scholars have debated Orwell's source of the dystopia. They need look no farther than Zamyatin's *We* (1921), which correctly predicted in nightmare detail the horrors to come under communist rule.

Consequently, although cordially invited to renew my Fulbright award with a choice of venue, I resigned shortly after returning home. The yearlong experience included many privileged moments, such as five-course dinners with my American friend, Bud Nafzger, who had retired from the State Department in order to teach, gratis, current events to interested Russian students. One night over chicken Kiev, he said that when he had attended a performance of Miller's *Death of a Salesman* as a young boy, his father, a tough Jewish lawyer from Queens, had pulled out his handkerchief and wept bitter tears at curtain call.

As the sole American-born literature scholar, I found myself much in demand: giving lectures, attending concerts, joining colleagues for literary discussions, and interviewing Fulbright candidates. Owing to my unique position as an American Fulbright with no competition, I never received a rejection slip. Still, I knew my limits, not to mention tolerance for a tightly closed society, so in June 1999, I said, "*Dasvidanya*, comrades! And thanks for the memories."

VIII.

Fire in the Belly

After all, my dear fellow, life, Anaxagoras has said, is a
journey.—Proust

In the spring of 1982, while scanning the shelves in a Riyadh bookstore, I came upon a brochure that offered summer courses in Arabic
for a reasonable tuition, plus room and board (one meal per day) in
Tunis, located near the Carthaginian ruins. I made a quick decision:
an intensive course might accomplish the well-known breakthrough,
since despite a year's formal/informal study, I was a slow language
learner. After filling out the registration form, I mailed the documents,
along with a banker's check in USD, and made flight arrangements
soon after collecting a princely sum at the cashier's office: a month's
pay plus summer wages.

In the downtown section of the capital, slabs of meat on public display hung by a length of rope to tempt passersby. The badly hacked
sections of beef, goat, or sheep were invariably black, not the red
color of raw meat. A thick coat of flies covered the cuts. If disturbed,
the insects formed a buzzing cloud and soon resettled. Open
sewage flowed sluggishly at intervals on the sidewalk. "Watch your
step!" was understood literally in the North African city. Also, the
word "odor" assumed a pungent meaning to contrast sharply with
"aroma."

The *Al-Madina Souq* presented a film *noir* setting starring Humphrey
Bogart, Peter Lorre, and Sidney Greenstreet wearing a fez. Approaching the bazaar, the tourist was beset by adolescent touts who guessed
with uncanny accuracy the nationality of a potential customer. They
offered a guided tour of Carthage, by then a crumbling ruin, and a

bargain on rugs, antiques, or leather goods, since a "cousin," "uncle," or close friend owned a nearby shop: "Special price. Small money, mister."

The male hustlers made lewd suggestions, producing pornographic prints, condoms, and sex toys displayed quickly, like an amateur magician's "now you see these forbidden wares, now you don't." Others dealt in bogus watches, cheap calculators, and bootleg cassettes of popular rock stars. And a few teens simply harassed tourists for money by displaying deformed limbs like Peachum's scoundrels in *Three Penny Opera*. One boy followed me, hand outstretched in supplication, with a fake limp. I turned sharply and said something in Arabic. He turned his back and shot a thrust kick, which I blocked, but the sharp edge of the heel struck my wrist painfully. Having been trained in the martial arts, I assumed a cat stance, and shouted *kiiia*! He laughed and skipped out of range.

I then resumed my way to the *souq* and noticed a tall, slender youth near a broken water fountain, which he guarded like an attack dog, glaring in my direction. His T-shirt, professionally printed in English, read, "Some night when you return home late, I'll be waiting. . ." A clear threat, though I did not take it personally. I glanced to my left, apprehensive, and thought, *Who would think of that menacing statement, print it for sale, and wear the shirt in public?*

Suddenly, I found myself in the *souq* and felt relieved. Hundreds of people, mostly foreigners, jostled one another like commuters on a New York subway. Despite the picturesque ambience inside the stone gate with its graceful arch, I found the conditions less than pristine along the maze of cobbled streets cluttered with handmade goods on offer. The narrow labyrinth, designed for pedestrians only, offered barely enough space for two-way passage.

At a fork deep in the market, I blundered into a large room strewn with luggage: some oiled and gleaming, others still under construction. The owner, seated at a bench festooned with tools and scraps, greeted me in demotic French. He was dressed in a traditional shift and wore a soiled skullcap. His full beard, flecked with grey, gave the impression of a chubby urchin peering through a thicket. With a grand sweeping gesture, he invited me to inspect his wares. "*Shoof*," he grunted. "*Momtaz.*"

Scanning the leather goods on display, I noticed a hand-tooled belt with Egyptian hieroglyphics carved into the leather, dyed blue, red, and yellow with black outlines. A scarab, symbol of immortality, was placed at the center, with several figures extending the length toward a heavy brass buckle. Kneeling, I examined the belt with child-like wonder. It was love at first sight. To be certain, I traced the hand-stitching for flaws. The work proved peerless; the intricate patterns and clean lines represented pride of craftsmanship. The length appeared right for my girth. No doubt something of a masterpiece, commanding a steep price. Still, I prepared to negotiate.

Before rising I unexpectedly felt pressure along my trapezoid muscle. Twisting my neck painfully, I saw the leather smith standing behind me, slightly bent and smirking. "*Nam? Nam?*" he asked, using the formal word for "yes." He wanted me to purchase the item, but we had not discussed the amount. That meant hard bargaining.

The hard sell annoyed me, but I wanted the belt, just not at the "tourist" price, since I had a sense of Tunisian economy. "*Becom?*" I enquired. "How much?"The owner quoted an astronomical number, even by Fifth Avenue standards. I concluded that I had misheard or forgotten the number system, which sometimes happened in moments of stress. "*Shuay, shuay,*" I replied. "Speak slowly." I had made no mistake; the wily merchant wanted over two hundred dollars USD.

Insulted, I rose to my feet and moved toward the door. The leather smith immediately halved the amount. I continued walking, and he again reduced the price by fifty percent. By then I was determined to leave, although the price was right. By the time I stepped over the threshold, however, the belt could have been mine for pocket change, but I did not break stride. Soon I exceeded shouting distance, though I had the distinct impression he wanted to pay *me* for the belt.

After a long morning in the *souq*, I felt hungry. Scores of teashops, authentic fast food joints predating McDonald's, Taco Bell, and Chicken Delight by centuries, honeycombed the market. The vendors, who were fluent in Arabic, French, and Spanish to accommodate the local/European trade, offered homemade-quality snacks: *falafel, hummus,* and *ful* (vegetable dishes); *kebab, shawarma,* and *kubideh* (meat course); yogurt, *baklava,* and *pistachios* (sweets). Those and other delicacies satisfied varied tastes and preferences; the snacks were unfailingly delicious, but the bland, spicy, or sweet recipes often came with a painful surcharge: gastroenteritis.

On an earlier occasion, to guarantee cleanliness and a delicious meal, I decided to dine at the luxurious Hotel Africa, which was modern and pristine. No respite: a large platter of *coos coos* with iced lemonade equaled a night of agony and dehydration. With that experience in mind, I chose my poison with some care. Stopping at a smiling vendor behind a shiny aluminum cart, I bought a fat gyro: thin slices of lamb doused with savory sauce and snuggled in pita bread. Before the first bite, a boy appeared with a wheelbarrow. It was loaded with chopped, melting ice—with various brands of soda lolling in the slush. I chose two cans of Pepsi, my favorite beverage, and tipped the lad before heading toward a scruffy rest area adjacent to the main thoroughfare. Seated on a boulder worn smooth by a million bottoms, I devoured the sandwich blissfully in the mottled shade of a ragged awning, riddled with holes like a fishnet.

Full, satisfied, and with renewed energy, I strode toward the entrance with purpose, maneuvering expertly through the pedestrians heading for the interior. Within sight of the entrance, I glanced upward and noticed, joined by white loom cords, two kilims draped over a dowel protruding from the rug shop's outside wall. A fat, jolly merchant lounged in the doorway. "Greetings," he shouted. "Welcome to my country. I am Mr. Abdullah. You can have anything, my friend. Special price." I replied in Arabic, *"Isme saeed Clifford, usteth coleeat adeb, gamiya Riyadh* [My name is Clifford, college of arts professor, Riyadh University"].

"*Qais! Doctor Cleeford,*" he said predictably. Pure flattery. I did not speak good Arabic on my most mellifluous day.

I pointed to the kilims and expressed interest. The owner disappeared into his shop, reappeared with a long pole, and expertly lowered the items to the ground. They were twins: identical in size and dyed overall a Maghreb scarlet, like arterial blood, with identical, abstract patterns in three contrasting tints. The classic example of a "conversation piece."

The rug merchant and I haggled in good faith and soon settled on a price. The owner again entered the shop and returned with a large clasp knife, which he snapped open. Grasping the blade in his right hand, Abdu sliced through the cords with a quick stroke. The rugs lay at my feet in the dust. As a matter of courtesy before claiming my prize, I handed Abdullah a wad of bills, and picked up the nearest rug. "*Ithnan!*" he exclaimed, seeing an easy mark. Clearly, he wanted to resume negotiations for the remaining carpet. "*La, wahed,*" I answered firmly. I didn't object to the price, but my small suitcase would accommodate only one kilim. Moreover, the customs agents, alert to opportunistic tariffs and fines, might enquire. Grinning, Abdullah stuffed the *filoos* uncounted into his *thobe* while I draped the rug like a serape over my left shoulder. We parted on good terms.

Only later I realized that the merchant had said "two" in an uncertain manner. Meaning I had actually paid for both rugs. However, I did not object to the arrangement. I had made a bargain, plus Abdullah and I, in the Middle East fashion, had become friends. In a tribal culture with little time for "developing relationships," a stranger was quickly regarded as either an ally or an enemy. As a case in point, my friend Jamil, in want of a wife, had arranged to meet a woman for the first time through a go-between in Jericho. He had arrived at the appointed hour bearing gifts. Upon the introduction, he announced, "I've come to propose!"

But I did not intend to conduct a study of the culture and cuisine, much less the sanitary conditions of the capital. As indicated above, I had matriculated at the Bourguiba Language Institute to polish my poor Arabic, which I had studied with a tutor in my office weekly and at the Riyadh Arabic Language Institute nightly. At that point, I had not arrived at the "learner's plateau"; in fact, although ritually praised by native speakers for my feeble efforts, I knew my command of pidgin Arabic required a great deal more classroom instruction and practice.

In order to pass the course and earn a certificate, however, I had to survive, which meant an existential choice: stop eating and drinking altogether or endure sleepless nights with stomach cramps, which in fact meant insufficient nutrition, since I could not keep anything down for long. Overweight for years despite diet and exercise, I had always hoped to lose some excess lard, but not by unintentional bulimia. I compromised by eating and drinking sparingly and with discretion. As I soon learned to my cost, however, self-delusion is without limit.

Still, three weeks into the term, I never missed a lesson, grinding my teeth along with my classmates and the Tunisian instructor during painful spasms. No one was spared the national plague. My apparent stoicism was partially explained by pride. Although my reading skills were lacking in comparison with those scholars who had taken university degrees in the classical language, my functional Arabic surpassed everyone in the class, save the native speaker. I therefore basked in the halo effect, since Ms. Sassi, who in fact affected a sassy manner, often called on me to show the class how it was done. Also, I chose among other options to study at the Tunis Institute, since the school taught a standard street Arabic: not slang, but removed from the Meccan dialect.

Colloquial expression was useful for those living and traveling in the Middle East. For reasons difficult to justify in pragmatic terms, formal courses almost invariably offered the Meccan dialect, which was no longer spoken except, like Renaissance academics who conversed in Latin, by highly educated professionals under special circumstances such as conference presentations. The reason for the above practice could be explained, somewhat convincingly, by the fact that dialects were so varied throughout the Middle East that even native speakers were sometimes stymied. Yet most understood Egyptian, Lebanese, Saudi, and Syrian variations. I had learned some Najdi, and when visiting other countries in the region, my interlocutors comprehended my feeble attempt to communicate—after a fashion.

Over the summer I made friends among my classmates. Brian, a plump tenor from the Deep South, entertained the class during break with arias from Italian operas. Christian, who planned to teach Arabic in Brittany, joined me each evening in the walled hotel garden to practice our lessons. Moreover, my colloquial Arabic earned me a "date" shortly after the midterm exam, which I passed handily. Megan, a comely young woman sitting next to me, had earned a BA in Arabic at Exeter.

She reminded me of a Lawrentian character, specifically the horse-dealer's daughter, although Megan had been born in Manchester, which was not rural. In fact, the city was identified with the industrial revolution and far removed from Lawrence country. During break one morning, she wondered if I would accompany her to a restaurant some evening. She stayed in a segregated dorm and confided, "The other girls are driving me quite mad." "Fine," I replied, "let's meet at the university bus stop about 7:15, and I'll take you to a place I know in the French quarter." She demurred, "But I want to speak Arabic." I laughed. "Don't worry. Everyone speaks it here, though educated professionals are bi-lingual. The cab driver and the waiter will speak the local dialect, guaranteed."

The casual dinner changed our summer plans drastically, and the evening at the restaurant was not without incident. The management had attempted a romantic ambience; a small candle burning fitfully in a rose-red glass encasement lit each table, just barely. The desired effect was somehow lost, however, giving the small dining room a Gothic, as opposed to a seductive, atmosphere. Yet the waiter was prompt, and the service exceeded the usual standard, which typically strained one's Western tolerance for cultural relativism.

The generous helpings featured several roasted vegetables, plus meat. Part way through meal, laced with warm conversation and *bon mots*, I cringed. At the edge of the plate—unbelievably—a human molar came into queasy focus in the flickering light. My stomach involuntarily heaved, and I turned to Megan with an innocuous remark in order to refocus. Surely a *trompe l'oeil*. Yet on second glance, the tooth remained *in situ*. To spare her sensibilities, I said nothing of the *hors d'oeuvre* to my dinner companion. Megan maintained a well-scrubbed, delicate appearance; she had never ventured outside Europe. Casually, I draped my napkin over the plate and motioned to the waiter, who promptly cleared the table. "But I wasn't finished," Megan mildly protested. "I know, but the sweets are rich and heavy. Better save some room."

At Megan's dorm near midnight, jasmine wafted from the courtyard, and tree frogs trilled from the garden. We agreed to sit together on the weekend tour bus. Virtually each Friday afternoon, the class boarded an air-conditioned coach in order to explore the ubiquitous Roman ruins, which attracted world travelers from Jordan to York—and many sites between. I took leave of Megan with an Arabic phrase. Nothing physical occurred between us, since I was her senior by more than twenty years; yet we were already close friends. In good spirits, I whistled off-key back to my room. Stripped to my soggy underwear, I slid gently into bed, face-down on the pillow, and slept peacefully. . .but not through the night.

Before dawn the curse struck, and I awoke with a start. Like Gradus, the Zambian assassin and Kinbote's nemesis, I felt bloated and wracked by the "inexhaustible lava in my bowels." An hour crept by painfully; no relief seemed possible. I was sick unto death by the long agony. The terror engulfing my stomach from the solar plexus to well below my navel came in waves, momentarily, with ever-increasing intensity. Writhing in bed until the cramps caused convulsions, I arose unsteadily and lurched to the nearby bathroom located just outside the door. My sleep cycle in shambles, night terror blended with night vision, and the room assumed a greenish hue, zebra-striped by dark shadows. My mouth went dry, my tongue swelled, restricting the acrid-tasting air. I wheezed like an old man with every strained breath. A shrill ringing sounded the alarm, but the source was not outside the open window, as I had first thought, but internal. Time stretched and collapsed like an accordion. Disoriented, I lost all sense of self. In a sweating, cold embrace with the tall specter of my uncanny Other, I silently screamed down a dark, haunted hallway. . .

By the next afternoon, lying sideways on the bed, I sensed someone moving about the room. Was I hallucinating as well? A young man's face came into focus. It was Christian, my study partner, who had spoken to Megan on the tour bus and learned that had I failed to show for the weekend trip. She was concerned. On Monday I missed class, so my study partner headed for the hotel, where the desk clerk gave him my room number. He bounded up the wide staircase, entered the room without knocking and found me astraddle the narrow bed, stripped to my briefs and soaked in sweat. Hearing my name, I came fully awake and realized several days had slipped by and not a mere twelve hours, according to my reckoning. My diaphragm ached, and I felt nauseous, groggy from lack of sleep. "I'll take you to the hospital," he announced. "My car is parked outside." He paused. "Don't worry, the clinic is free. Socialism!" he stated, with smug expression. "Where are your clothes?" he asked. "I'll help you get dressed."

A short drive maneuvering through heavy traffic, horns blaring, and we passed the open gate without the usual guard on duty. One of us remembered the Arabic for "Visitor Parking." Inside the clinic, which was empty except for an intern, I sat on a gurney moaning softly while the bearded young man prepared a syringe. Without knowing my tolerance for hard drugs, he told me to lower my trousers before plunging a needle the size of a spike from a get-well-card cartoon deep into my *gluteus maximus* and pressed the plunger. Instantly, I understood why drug addicts stopped at nothing for a fix: euphoria. Money, fame, love, sex, and success meant nothing. It was not peace, as in the Vietnam-era phrase, but "Paradise now!"

Later, while nodding out, a radiologist speaking Parisian French guided me to the X-ray room, where I was declared free of ulcers and stomach cancer. My bowels were inflamed, but otherwise free of irregularities. The doctor mixed powder with water, and within minutes I walked out of the hospital holding a week's supply of the panacea, a pain-free and happy man: deliverance at no charge. Perhaps I had underestimated the virtues of socialist medicine, after all. In any case, I decided to abstain from food and drink, except for bottled water sold at the hotel pharmacy, until I cleared customs for the flight to London, where I could enjoy the remaining summer break in comfort.

The following day I skipped class. At noon, I found Megan in the tea garden. She had been spared the gastric ordeal and looked quite content. She had come to a decision. "Cliff, I realized after dinner last week that I am wasting my time. I can't speak Arabic, so I'm leaving on Wednesday." She had a point. "What about your graduate program and language scholarship?" I asked. "Well, I have a minor in Medieval history, so I'll just change my topic," she said matter-of-factly. "Oh," she added, "and you can get a certificate of attendance, since you worked past the midterm. Proves you studied here." I welcomed the information. "Well, can't hurt. Thanks for the information." She sipped her tea. "Are you leaving, too, then?" About to answer, I had a thought. "Yeah, but I have decided, just now in fact, to visit Athens. Since early childhood, I have always wanted to see the ancient ruins, plus I was married for ten years, and I acquired a natural inclination for Greek tragedy," I said, laughing. We parted with a warm hug and promised to keep in touch. I never heard from Megan again.

At the travel agency, a short walk from my hotel, I bought a ticket without using English, though I overheard the clerk speaking my native tongue on the phone. I packed that night, slept well, and headed for the airport a full hour early. The plane left on schedule and with no stopovers on the flight from Tunis to Athens, I settled in for a short hop. After we reached altitude, the attendant provided a snack with a soft drink. I then dozed for an hour and refreshed from a short nap, caught up on the news with a complimentary copy of *USA Today*. A few minutes later, we prepared to land. I was euphoric. Thanks to the healing powder, my digestion felt normal, and I had lost thirty pounds. Moreover, I fantasized the ancient enquiry: As a traveling scholar, I would continue the classical dialectic in the *Agora*, a public expression of doctrine without a fee—the Socratic ideal in the late twentieth century realized at last.

IX.

"It's All Greek to Me"

The Lord whose oracle is at Delphi neither reveals nor
conceals, but gives a sign.—Heraclitus

After a difficult year in Saudi Arabia's culturally sterile, police state
and painful bouts of gastroenteritis in Tunis, I decided to visit Athens,
which exceeded my great expectations. On the cab ride from the airport, sun-bleached Doric columns stood—dreamlike—among the
cypress and fir trees lining the road. Peering from the taxi, I embraced
the distant past, which invoked nostalgia for the present. Textbooks,
photographs, films, and lectures not withstanding, only the empirical
evokes magic. The ruined legacy of classical civilization and cradle of
democracy recalled Pallas Athene, the capital city's Olympian
patroness, who had wielded great power.

As goddess of wisdom and war, she had offered a pagan complement
for the omniscient/omnipotent deity of monotheism in its avatars of
Judaism, Christianity, and Islam. She had embodied a catalogue of
virtues, including courage, strength, justice, and strategy. Her pagan
worshippers had looked to Athena for inspiration in mathematics and
the arts, as well as for increased technical skills. She had reigned over
philosophy. Moreover, the parthenogenetic warrior had been a goddess of civilization itself, on which humans had depended. For, as
Aristotle observed in *Politics*: "Anyone who either cannot lead the
common life or is so self-sufficient as not to require community, and
therefore does not partake of society, is either a beast or a god."

The epithet "bright-eyed" associates Athena with the keen-sighted owl,
her totem animal, that only flies at night to enlighten mankind with
philosophy and wisdom. With a background in classical literature and
culture, I felt welcome, a rich sense of *nostos*: the homecoming.

The city center, built on high ground, developed over the centuries into a modern metropolis, allowing the outer reaches, except for scattered ruins, to disappear: a testament to their former glory. I concluded that Athens deserved the title Eternal City, which had been usurped by her conqueror, Rome. The stately pillars that stood like sentinels in the wooded slopes stretching to the water's edge below, failed to prepare one adequately for the shock of recognition: the Parthenon, a privileged sight from the Plaka—Athens' tourist quarter crowded with cheap apartments, curio shops, and small restaurants. Sacred to Athena Parthenos (the virgin), that monument, built on the Acropolis ("above the city"), gave the capital its distinct ever-present character, and the magnificent temple was lit at night, shining like a beacon. The ruins offered an unparalleled landmark, enhancing a casual stroll through the narrow streets, a simple meal while dining *al fresco*, and a room with a view.

After booking a room, I explored the *Agora*: the open market where Socrates had engaged in dialectic with his young students. The wise old man, delinquent in the mission to buy food staples for his family, had practiced a unique pedagogy without fee or texts and most importantly, in *public*, making it virtually impossible to profess subversive doctrine. Socrates had required no entrance exam, and all had been welcome. Seeking wisdom, he had enquired of public figures, as well, and had soon concluded that their pretended knowledge proved of little value. He then made his views public, resulting in his execution. Generations later, his intellectual grandson Aristotle, while under similar threat, had chosen voluntary exile, so that Athens might not sin twice against philosophy.

Like Buddha, Jesus, and Mohammed, the sage of Athens had left no written record. He preferred lengthy discourse on crucial topics like justice, politics, language, beauty, love, and suicide—enquiries which extend to the present. The dialectic sought clarity, as opposed to conclusion, and ended temporarily at a moment of uncertainty: the Socratic *aporia*, literally "no way" forward.

Gazing on shapeless debris, I reflected on his corrected wording of the Sophist dictum: "The unexamined statement is not worth making."

Rather, Socrates had pronounced, "The unexamined *life* is not worth living." In parallel fashion, he had practiced the Delphic inscription *gnōthi seauton*: "Know thyself." Throughout his short tenure as unpaid headmaster (what sensible professor undercuts his employer's convictions in the classroom?), Socrates had examined his pupils in the ideal universe of discourse.

With those thoughts in mind, I lighted a *puro* and, sitting on a convenient slab, recalled his pointed question concerning one's obligation to the "they," who anonymously judge and control our public behavior: "But why, my dear Crito, should we be concerned with the opinion of the many?" His interlocutor had opined that "they" could do harm, to which Socrates had replied that for good or ill, the many only affected us by *tuché*: chance.

Light headed on a Platonic high, I left the Agora and followed a group of Japanese sightseers, well fortified with Nikons, to the cliffside path, which led to the temple. After a steep climb, I beheld the Parthenon in its majesty; a crowd flowed toward the colonnade, so many. I had not thought the touts had led so many. There I saw one I knew and stopped him, crying "Moodie, you were with me at the Tea Garden in Riyadh." Mahmoud "Moodie" Hourani, my former colleague, turned and said, "Indeed," while vigorously shaking hands in the Saudi fashion, "and how is your Arabic?" I gathered my thoughts and replied, "Better, after the trip to North Africa; otherwise I would have been stranded first in Heliopolis and then in Tunis after the plane touched down." My colleague chuckled, "Right, immersion is your only man."

Well met, we toured the palatial grounds and ventured inside, overwhelmed by the immensity of the interior and humbled at the statues larger than life. Moodie said, "Listen, mate, my bird stood me up, and I have an extra ticket for island hopping. Would you like to join me on an excursion?" I hesitated. "Well, I'm not much for hopping. I get sea sick, but I suppose a short cruise out and back the same day would be fun." Moodie suggested, "Let's tuck in first. I know a lovely garden restaurant near the dock. After dinner, we'll board the next boat to Aegina, a brilliant day trip." Mentally, I checked my stash of Greek drachma. "Let me stop by the room first," I said. "We'll hail a cab to Piraeus, and I'll spring for the chow."

Seated among the olive trees, we chose three dishes each from the menu: *avgolemono*, *moussaka*, and *baklava* (my choice); *fassolatha*, *pastitsio*, and *galaktoboureko* (Moodie's preference). "And I recommend the pizza," Dr. Hourani announced with authority. "You must be joking," I replied. Then I added, "Don't forget I grew up just across the Hudson and lived for a time in the Big Apple. I've had primo pizza all my life on Forty Second Street, the best, at the Blue Hill Country Club in New Jersey, and not to mention The Crow's Nest in Ashtabula, when I lived in Ohio." Moodie rolled his eyes and pronounced, "Try the specialty here. You won't be disappointed."

In the event, I took my friend's suggestion. When the second course arrived, I sampled a slice and conceded: one of the best pies ever, starting with the all-important crust: thin, moist, and crunchy; covered with a thick layer of melted cheese, sliced tomato, and mushrooms; well garnished with black olives; and of course, glistening with extra virgin olive oil. Moodie washed down the meal with the local red wine, while I guzzled Pepsi, the universal soft drink and my caffeine fix since 1943. With minutes to spare, we toasted our upcoming sea journey with *ouzo*, sticky sweet and sharp to the tongue and palate.

The gods smiled during the short voyage to our destination. Despite a boiling Aegean sun, we were spared the predictable slow bake by a light, tangy breeze, and owing to a calm sea, I kept down the meal. An unexpected bonus: as the island with its white beaches loomed, the young women on board, like mythic sea nymphs, crowded to the bow and stripped to the buff. My colleague, who had spent his impressionable years in the repressive Middle East, gasped at the sight of plump behinds, which were soon covered, just barely, by bikinis, appearing like a magician's rabbit from bulging handbags. We made eye contact, and I grinned with barely suppressed lust. "I say that's a bit off," he muttered. With an opportunity to take the rise in English fashion, I replied, poker-faced, "After such voyeurism, what forgiveness?"

The free show proved to be the highlight of the trip, as the island offered little save an idyllic walking tour of a quaint village. After strolling the cobbled streets for an hour, I was ready to return. Moodie decided to embark on another voyage, so we shook hands again and promised to keep in touch. *"Ma'salaama, ya akhi,"* he said quietly. *"Arak fil djenna,"* I replied, knowing full well that "See you in Paradise" was inappropriate. I was an infidel, and the expression meant that one or both companions didn't expect to survive an upcoming crisis, like a suicide mission.

After a night of troubled sleep, tormented by mosquitoes, I awoke early, checked out of the low-rent apartment, and booked a spacious hotel room overlooking Constitution Square. A quick milkshake at the hotel coffee shop, and I headed for the nearby tourist center, where I purchased a round-trip ticket to Epidaurus, the still-functioning outdoor Dionysian theatre located a lengthy bus ride outside the city. Once on board I engaged in conversation with Fernando Rodriquez, a Classics scholar conducting research on *Troades*, the sole extant and final drama of Euripides' trilogy. Anticipating an evening production by torchlight of *The Trojan Women*, he spoke of *hamartia*, *peripeteia*, *denouement*, and *catastrophe* in the assured tone of well-prepared authority. With little Latin and less Greek, I felt assured of better understanding the production, translated into modern Greek expression from an ancient, literary dialect.

When the driver announced Arcadia, a disappointing, barren stretch far removed from the Persian vision of a lush, eternal park, Dr. Rodriguez murmured, *"Et in Arcadia ego* [And I, too, was in Paradise]"—the medieval *memento mori* portrayed graphically in Guercino's painting (1638), reminding believers that Death was omnipresent and without boundaries. Freshly apprised of my mortality, I replied, "Thus, *carpe diem ad infinitum* [Seize the day eternally], my friend."

Having both passed the forty milestone, we chuckled sardonically, in full view of the fact that both the theater and the tragedy, still vital, had lasted more than two thousand years, while we had begun the final, unrehearsed act.

Unexpectedly, we stopped briefly to visit a site that hosted summer games, where naked athletes struggled to honor—though not compete with—the jealous gods, who observed the annual *agon* from the snow-covered mountain, Olympus, which ironically had outlasted the immortals by some two millennia. Nearby, several hundred years before the birth of Christ, a Delphic priestess had responded to specific questions with ambiguous answers misinterpreted by self-serving searchers, who invariably (like Shakespeare's Macbeth) found succor and confidence in prophecy—but no satisfaction in misunderstood destiny. Socrates alone had known that the pronouncement "None is wiser than Socrates" meant he understood human limitations. I approached the crevice and murmured, "How long do I live?" In the distance I heard, hauntingly, an owl call, but no answer to my fateful question.

Our bus to Epidaurus arrived at twilight, an hour before the performance and with ample opportunity to explore the nearby ruins: housing, library, baths, and the shrine of Asclepius, god of healing. According to Aristotle, tragedy combined fear and pity had produced an emotional purge; that is, the annual Dionysian theater festival provided both entertainment and emotional cleansing. While touring the site, Professor Rodriquez observed, "You know, Cliff, people spend a small fortune at theme parks—a few hours of thrill rides, a shooting gallery, side show, hot dogs, cotton candy, and pure kitsch. Here, for the price of a fast-food snack, you get a tour of classical sites and ruins, a genuine performance in the original theatre. It's the whole package."

Moments later we followed busloads of passengers, who had been arriving steadily all evening, into the amphitheater that had been sculpted by corvée labor into the canyon rock. The magnificent auditorium was not beautiful as advertised in travel brochures, but sublime as understood by Kant. Mighty cataracts, the starry heavens, vast murals, for example, exceeded the empirical capacity/attendant emotions, and one could not grasp fully the transcendent moment, leaving the viewer (often literally) breathless. Oval tiers accommodated more than 13,000 patrons. Its acoustics, as often noted, were without parallel; a cough, finger snap, or rustle would, like a Hollywood stereophonic system, sound near at hand throughout. Whispered secrets were made instantly public. The theatre confirmed the democratic ideal, for all seats were equal, and one chose a perfect spot to view the performance by whim—though in classical times, priests and officials occupied the reserved top rows.

With a lighting of torches at rear stage, the performance began, a studied costume dance in a foreign tongue made manifest through a glass darkly in flickering half-light. Time froze while dark figures moved eerily in the distance. Having read and taught Euripides' masterpiece in the Western Literature survey course, I followed the plot without difficulty, while my better-prepared colleague occasionally nodded in understanding at crucial lines. During certain scenes we made eye contact, and I knew his meaning: dramatic irony, foreshadowing, tragic epiphany. A moment of intensity occurred shortly before the formal climax (the burning of Troy, which was not performed on stage): a council of Greek Ancients decided that Hector's son, Astyanax, must be put to death. Our cultural ancestors were nothing if not pragmatic, reasoning that the innocent child, playing happily with his grandmother, might have grown to manhood fixed on revenge. Talthybias lifted the boy gently and walked grimly to the exit portal, stage right. A moment of synchronicity: as Agamemnon's herald of arms crossed the threshold, a flutter of bats, on cue, swooped above the lintel—the entrance to Hades, the all-embracer. As a seasoned theatre patron, I experienced a new dimension at Epidaurus: literally stage-struck as ancient and modern bonded.

Later, torches snuffed, the audience sat for a moment in darkness, a haunting chant emanating from the occult entrance. Fernando and I walked in silence to the parking area. As I turned to board the Athens bus, my colleague clapped me firmly on the shoulder. "I made arrangements to spend the night in the village," he said quietly. "It's been real, and it's been nice," and he added with a grin, "Been real nice meeting you, *maestro*." "Same here," I replied, "and *adios, amigo*," in unison.

As the door whooshed open, I climbed the steps and headed to the backseat, where I sprawled and dozed until city lights awoke me. I bought a chocolate bar and soda at a kiosk before turning in for the night, tired but utterly relaxed in the afterglow of the stunning, unforgettable performance—fixed like the imprinted moment after birth.

The following morning I arranged a trip to London; after Manhattan, it was my favorite city for bookshops, restaurants, theatre, and adventure. I booked a three-star hotel in the West End, which satisfied the above criteria. During the next two days, I relaxed in the approved tourist fashion: read *Zorba the Greek* by Kazantzakis over a dish of dried calamari with a glass of *retsina* in the Plaka; bought, along with the customary postcards and trinkets, an obligatory striped fisherman's shirt; and feasted on seafood at a seaside table, where waiters skillfully dodged traffic, never missing a step or dropping a loaded tray. Packing quickly, I savored a final, visual embrace of the Parthenon guarding the classical city. I then flagged a cab to the airport and caught the last plane to London, which departed at sunset. Like Athena's owl, I "took flight. . .when the shades of night were falling. . ."

X.

Pound Foolish

When I was one-and-twenty
I heard a wise man say,
"Give pounds and crowns and guineas
But not your heart away. . ." — A. E. Houseman,

The taxi driver at Heathrow Airport saluted. "Where to, guv?" He drove me, with the certainty of a sleepwalker, straight to the door of the President Hotel in the West End. As the cabbie proudly stated, he'd spent nearly three years pedaling a two-wheeler in order to acquire the knowledge: a cognitive map of London's labyrinthine streets, lanes, and byways. He knew each turn and cul de sac, adding that the city of "Londinium," with its original unpaved paths, stretched back to early 50 AD. By Chaucer's era, the metropolis had already been a millennium in the making. A confident command of "one of the dark places on earth" proved no mean accomplishment; my cabbie never missed a turn.

At the destination I pressed a wad of notes, which covered the expensive fare plus a generous tip, in the driver's large hand—for the ride and good company. Finally, thanks to petro dollars, I had enough money to reward properly those who worked hardest and most productively. "Cheers, mate," he exclaimed as he shoved the dosh uncounted into his purse.

Inside the lobby I approached the front desk, surplus quid in hand. London hotels were by then demanding a cash advance, after a series of "sleep and runners" had eroded trust. The lift door opened, emitting a lone passenger, chuckling. I would have recognized the high-pitched laugh anywhere. It was Dr. Jerry King, a Saudi colleague who had left Riyadh earlier. We noted the coincidence of an unplanned meeting, not the first or last moment of synchronicity that informed our long friendship and later correspondence. I counted the chance meeting with Jerry as a good omen, setting a positive tone for the adventures ahead.

Room key in hand, I ascended three floors to unpack, shower, and recount my spending money, a considerable sum. I was in fact loaded, having just arrived from a teaching assignment in Riyadh, Saudi Arabia. Despite many drawbacks, foreign workers like myself benefited by large, tax-free salaries, complemented by benefits, which included medical/dental services, internal transportation allowance, and an annual plane ticket. After the initial year instructing undergraduate scholars in Western literature and criticism, I had finally hit the jackpot: my final month's salary and benefits package, summer pay, plus a conference stipend and a fee to edit their in-house journal.

Having previously visited London in 1968 with only a few pence to my name, I was anxious to compensate for tramping the streets down and out like Orwell and make extravagant use of my discretionary funds. I would play the last of the big spenders from the East for a London summer and indulge myself like an Oriental despot. In fact, I sent postcards with a single alliterative phrase: "Landed in London, living large!" The aesthetic stage, according to Kierkegaard, characterizes childhood, when sensual delight directs interest and behavior; the adult mode, if feeling (as opposed to thinking) predominates, combines physical and intellectual stimulation. Consciously, then, I chose a period of regression.

After a hot shower and solid nap, I awoke just before noon. Seated in the elegant dining room, I ordered bangers and mash, baked beans, buttered toast and jam with a large pot of tea. I elected to skip the dessert, as my stomach was bulging over my belt line after a year of binging in Riyadh. Daily there I'd feasted on *schawarma* sandwiches, *hummus*, *kabsa*, yellow dates washed down with *laban*, and Pepsi. Each

Friday evening, I had gormandized at the Airport Street Hilton, which had offered a weekly buffet.

Eager to visit favorite London haunts, I crossed Russell Square at a leisurely pace, admiring the spring blooms of Bloomsbury. Then a rangy panhandler unexpectedly blocked my path. The homeless man appeared disheveled, inebriated; his muscular arms were covered with nautical tattoos and crisscrossed with a network of veins. He cocked his head and made his pitch. "Look, mate, I swear to sweet Jesus I'd stick me own mother for a pint. Could you help out an old sea dog on his uppers?" Instinctively, I glanced at his right hand, anticipating the glint of steel. He was unarmed. "How much for a couple of rounds?" I enquired. "Just enough for a game of darts, old shipmate," he said. I ignored the deceptive response and produced a five-pound note. "Will this do?" I asked. "Right. Thanks, lad. You're a good bloke." He took the money, made an about-face, and quick marched toward the nearest pub.

I left the park and headed for Charing Cross Road, where quaint bookstores abounded, their cramped and crooked shelves haunted by bibliophiles of past ages. I imagined Dr. Johnson with his faithful Boswell perusing thick tomes, at ease in their bookish world. I cracked a few texts and read the opening passages, checking for style. Eventually, I settled for a slim volume of poetry, which I slipped into my outside jacket pocket. The proprietor placidly smoked a gnarled briar pipe, oblivious to customers, while he scanned a yellowed newspaper reporting the catastrophes of another era. Discreetly, I placed a crisp tenner on the counter and left the shop.

Impulsively, I decided to spend the afternoon slumming and struck out for Soho, the London tenderloin. By the late 1960s, the Lord Chamberlain, England's official censor, had lost his punch. Risqué plays, films, and novels had flourished. Over the following decades, writers could publish the most outrageous scenarios without fear of censorship, though strict libel laws were still enforced. The obscene image, however, remained relatively proscribed. With the hope of finding the real thing, Soho beckoned.

Upon entering an adult bookstore on Greek Street, the owner greeted me effusively. "We got what you want, mate. Don't be shy. Take your time. Loops downstairs for 50p: spanking the maid, French, the odd knee-trembler. Separate booths, private-like. A bit nice for wankers." Ignoring the hard sell, I riffled through a slick magazine called "Bare Birds," featuring full-bosomed young ladies in lascivious poses: soft core at best, with the more promising publications sealed in plastic. "Got your eye on those fannies, sir. Two mags, anyone you like, for a quid. Fair enough?" Annoyed by false promises and frustrated, I abruptly turned toward the door. "I've seen a lot better in Denmark, twenty years ago," I said sarcastically.

The owner blanched. "Wait here. Don't stir!" he gasped. Producing a brass key, he unlocked a nearby storeroom and disappeared, slamming the door. A sliver of light limned the entrance. He soon returned grasping a sheaf of 8x10 glossies. Like a practiced casino dealer, he began placing the photos, one by one, on the counter for my inspection. He was livid with rage. "Look at that! Just look," he fumed. "That's the real fuckin' suck, mate. The real suck!"

As a teenager, I had first scanned illicit dirty pictures pilfered from drawers and distributed among friends: prints, realistic illustrations, cartoons. By middle age, I considered myself an old hand—a worldly fellow familiar with all manner of smut. However, as I glanced in awe at the photographs, I blushed. Terms like "XXX" and "hardcore" seemed insufficient. Admittedly, the diminutive Cockney shopkeeper, a Dickensian caricature with requisite bushy eyebrows, bulgy eyes, and muttonchops had called my bluff. *There* was printed porn in the raw.

Like a public schoolboy caught smugging by the headmaster, I avoided eye contact and left quickly, with the dwarfish owner calling plaintively, "Hold on, china. I've got something to your taste—caning, bondage, leather. Take a gander, if you like."

Back on the street, I was temporarily disoriented and lost my bearings, stumbling onto a card game. I had assumed three-card Monte had been invented on Manhattan's Forty Second Street, but I was wrong. British counterparts had set up a table surrounded by a gaggle of gullible tourists with a few tough shills. Nothing new under the sun: the old shell game replaced by cards. A heavyset man dealing the bent cards saw me coming, the next fat mark—and a Yank to boot. As fresh meat, I was up for the chop.

Fascinated by an "easy" game that players never win, I joined the onlookers. A rugged man with a flat nose tried his luck. He chose the wrong card. Of the three possibilities, the elusive ace squatted to the left, not in the middle, as the hapless punter had miscalculated. He faced me with a grim expression, breathing beer fumes. "The cunt keeps moving the prize," he said angrily. "When time to bet, put your finger on the one I say." Expertly, the con artist arranged the cards once more. "This one," the phony gambler said, pointing, "for two," and I stabbed the middle card with a forefinger, pinning his choice to the table. The dealer turned the card: Ace!

Without a word, he paid his partner and pealed off fifty-pound notes from a thick wad. Leaning forward, he offered the unearned sum, enough to tempt a Buddhist saint. Shaking my head slowly, I refused the money. I knew that the expectant "winner" would lose all, since the bait actually never reached the sucker. At the precise moment of accepting the ill-gotten gain, a serpent strike would empty the gull's inside pocket, and the dipper would take his leave. Should a loser bent on assault choose to follow the thief, the pickpocket and his associates were well prepared for any contingency, boxing/wrestling skills and stealthy clasp knives at the ready. "Nothing to do with me," I croaked. "Don't let him cheat you out of it, mate," another shill advised. Time to split. I brushed passed the assistant who had set me up and left the area, wallet/passport intact.

Ravenous and parched, I made my way toward Leicester Square and stopped at the Comedy Carnival pub for refreshment. The barkeep, a tall reedy Irishman, pointed to the empty stool near the taps. "What you'll be having, then?" he enquired. "Give me a wee drop of The Macallan, splash of water, and shepherd's pie," I answered.

After a long boozy chat with the bartender, who rehearsed the history of the Troubles, I staggered out, leaving a small pile of change on the counter and invoking the notion that a rich man like myself couldn't be bothered with clinking coins, which were heavy in the pocket and chafed my plump thigh with each stride. Hailing a cab, I headed back to my hotel. I evaluated my first day as the prodigal son: exciting, satisfying, and worth every copper.

Looking back, I spent lavishly throughout that self-indulgent London summer. The fabled fog never occurred, nor did it rain often. I smoked Monte Christos, bought a hand-knit woolen sweater for my son, ate often at the upscale Carvery, attended Hollywood matinées and the West End theatre at night—never counting the cost. By September, with a chill in the air, I enjoyed a final Devon tea with clotted cream, raspberry jam, and scones in an upscale shop across from Harrods. After a brilliant tea, while puffing a mellow cigar, I reflected on wealth—its benefits and consequences. Certainly, excess bank notes provided a unique sense of independence, freedom from anxiety, well-being. What if it were to dissipate, however—which was not unusual in the age of uncertainty. Would I steal, cheat, lie, betray those who trusted my word in order to ensure an indefinite season of profligate spending? Was a fat bank account, along with substantial investments, worth more than friendship, self-respect, peace of mind? I thought not.

I had not been put to a severe test, but felt confident I would have refused the Devil's pact and slept well, regardless. The accumulation of wealth beyond comfort and relative security did not and does not consume my thoughts or define my passion. Yet I often recall that summer of easy living in London as a privileged respite from financial worry: pleasant, carefree, and aesthetically gratifying, certainly—but not priceless.

XI.

A City by the Black Sea

Treasure the dream, whatever the terror.—*Gilgamesh*

Rose Macaulay's fabled towers of Trebizond (now Trabzon) are no more, and the city has turned its back on the sea, once a major port connecting the Silk Road. Traveling by bus, a smoke-filled room without a view, Andrew Arrowsmith and I arrived in late afternoon after a sleepless night on the road—hacking, red-eyed, hungry, and exhausted. Upon de-boarding, Andrew wanted first to stop at an antiquities shop nearby. Then to supper. As a first time visitor, I suggested we go by foot in order to absorb the local color, much to the chagrin of several boisterous cabbies who vied for our custom. "Right," he agreed, "we can use the exercise."

My new English colleague, fluent in Turkish and with degrees in Near East history and archeology, had spent six years in Anatolia on the Mediterranean coast. He had taught humanities and English at the local high school, supervised two digs outside Cappadocia, and published a number of scholarly articles in British journals. We had met in the Bilkent University faculty lounge soon after I had returned from Syria over the *bayram* [winter break] and had immediately exchanged travel stories. "Have you by chance ever been north, to the Black Sea?" he had asked. "I haven't visited any of the in-country sites, not even Istanbul or the ruins of Troy on the Dardanelles," I had replied. "In a fortnight we'll go to Trabzon, marvelous city, for the long weekend," he had suggested. And so we had made arrangements.

The Trabzon bus depot was located in a seedy area resembling a sepia, turn-of-the-century postcard. In keeping with the milieu, "Ahmed's Golden Lamp," owned by a heavy-set importer whose jowls for religious convictions never felt steel, met Dickensian expectations: a fantasy of artifacts, coins, figurines, tribal rugs, and bric-a-brac. There, after sharp bargaining, the discerning collector might have decorated his den with exotica at Depression-era prices.

Ahmed, misreading us as gullible tourists, sensed an opportunity, and as an opening gambit, he presented a matched pair of Roman amphorae encrusted with lime, salt, and dead barnacles. I glanced at Andrew, who confirmed the jars' authenticity: the genuine item. Out of curiosity, I asked in Turkish, "How much?" The offering price might have tempted a museum curator with deep pockets, but the amount exceeded my ability to calculate in Turkish lira. Moreover, without proper documentation, the naïve tourist attempting to transport the jars out of the country risked a Turkish prison sentence for making off with a national treasure—two, in fact.

We took a pass on a fertility goddess with multiple, bulging breasts: worth a small fortune if genuine, which it was clearly not. Next, Ahmed barked a sharp command to an assistant, who darted into the back room. He reappeared with a large tribal rug, which he unrolled for our inspection. The Caucasian kilim showed wear and the original blood-red dye had faded to tea rose, a blushing pink. Neither of us bothered to count the knots—not worth the effort. As we moved toward the door, Andrew turned and exchanged a few words in Turkish, thanked the owner, and announced, "Right, we will eat and kip straight away, mate."

Passing a small bakery with streaked, paint-chipped shop windows, I stopped and exclaimed with barely controlled enthusiasm, "Hey, man, look: Napoleons!" I had not savored a genuine *mille-feuille* [thousand leaves] pastry since 1955, when I would sometimes spend my lunch money (50¢) on the custard-and-chocolate-icing delicacy. In the usual capitalist fashion, the authentic recipe, which required three days for preparation, had become compromised, starting with frozen puff pastry and completing the culinary catastrophe with processed, chemically enhanced chocolate spooned from a jar.

We each bought a heavy slice wrapped in wax paper and slipped gently into a small paper bag. "Dessert!" I announced, as we quickened our pace up a gentle slope to the Al-Gulsha Hotel.

Seated at a large, badly scarred table, Andrew ordered the traditional thin-sliced lamb dish awash in melted butter, a Julienne salad loaded with fresh seafood, a side of red pepper-feta hummus, and with Coke to drink, the sole item I could read on the menu. The comely waitress, with no top button to her bulging peasant blouse, kept smiling at my friend and asking pointedly if he wanted anything else, anything at all. I spoke barely functional Turkish, so I asked my interpreter companion to keep me in the conversational loop. "What did she mean by that?" I asked innocently. "What do you think she meant?" he answered dryly. I have always preferred understated British wit uttered with a sly smirk to brash American punch lines accompanied with unearned laughter by the would-be standup comedian himself.

When the meal arrived promptly with more smiles at my shipmate, we tucked in with gusto. At a nearby table, six or seven locals sipped scalding Turkish coffee, talking in deep tones and chuckling among themselves. An imposing young man with a Germanic dueling scar opened a full pack of cigarettes by tearing off the entire top portion and offered the contents to his friends, who eagerly reached for the jolt of flavored nicotine. Matches flared, the smell of sulfur and then tobacco fumes further polluted the eye-watering dining room, which already resembled a smokehouse. The mild spring temperature notwithstanding, the restaurant windows remained sealed shut. "Not again," I moaned, referring to the TB-inducing bus ride. "Right," Andrew agreed, "the Turks like nothing better than to sit around in an air-tight room and smoke up a nice funk." I reflected for a moment. "Now I know why our Turkish friends don't make it much past fifty," I observed. "If not early roadkill, the big 'C' ensures that few reach a ripe old age." Andrew replied, "Remember, mate, it's in the hands of Allah: kismet."

After the lightly-smoked meal topped by our rich pastry, we approached the downstairs check-in counter, where Andrew rented separate rooms furnished with a single narrow cot and little else. The 60-watt bulb barely illuminated the film *noir* interior, shabbily furnished and so cramped, as the vaudevillian remarked, "You had to go out in the hall in order to change your mind." I removed my shoes and windbreaker before climbing between the cool, dank sheets. Some hours later, scuttling across the wooden floor awakened me. "Just rats," I whispered and turned over to await the ragged dawn.

With no shower and no delay getting dressed, we paid the bill, collected our passports, and headed for a three-star hotel two narrow streets closer to the Black Sea. Andrew briefly spoke to the manager, who kept shaking his head in disapproval. While climbing the stairs, he told me that the hotel did not allow professional discounts. "Does any establishment?" I asked. "Well, I'm a bit of a chancer," he replied. "Sometimes it works." The generic house key, which did not inspire confidence, opened a narrow door lacking a fresh coat of paint to one large room furnished with two king-size beds, a clean bathroom with tub and shower, fat Turkish towels, and a large bowl of complimentary fruit. "You wash up first," I said, reaching for a ripe pear from the cornucopia on the dresser. "I'm going to hit the rack and fill the tub for a bath later." I then stripped to my briefs and wife-beater shirt, peeled back the comforter, and virtually passed out as my head hit the pillow.

Some hours later, I opened my eyes briefly to catch TV images, a late-night movie with subtitles. Andrew, on the sunny side of early middle age, spent the night as a premature Sundowner with little discretion: re-runs, games shows, heavily edited pornography, propaganda in the guise of news casts, infomercials—all worth his attention well after the witching hour. I groaned, turned over, and slept the sleep of the just—or at least the very tired.

I awoke shortly before noon to Andrew wearing a dragon-skin like an Oriental pasha and surrounded with apple cores, peach pits, and orange peels littering the bedspread. He closed a volume of Gibbon's history in the miniscule Everyman edition. He vowed to complete the masterpiece, unabridged, before turning forty—and his next birthday was approaching.

"Get much rest?" I asked sarcastically. Meeting my gaze, Andrew invoked *The Big Sleep*. "No offense," he added, "but you snore like an elephant." I did not mention the soporific text on the decline and fall, always an appropriate theme in the former Ottoman Empire, and the comment on my fumed-induced sinus condition. "Where to?" I asked hopefully. Slipping the volume into his bulging pocket, he replied, "Last time I visited the tomb, Ataturk's villa, and the castle, so I enquired about the Sumela monastery, which is located a few miles from here. The workers' van leaves from the waterfront every hour or so. We can ride with them. At the last stop, the driver will take us the rest of the way and wait. Just a few quid."

I hopped out of bed and padded to the bathroom. "Be right with you, buddy," I called as the water from both taps thundered into the tub. In one of Austen's novels, a character remarks of a spa, "I have heard the waters there are not unhealthful." Exactly. A deep soak revives the mind and the body in equal measure. Fifteen minutes later, shampooed, shaved, and refreshed, we marched like palace guards through the narrow streets toward the sea.

Our timing, in sync with the departure schedule, meant precious little room. The vehicle was packed to the gunnels with heavy smokers, the side windows tightly shut. The driver soon cleared the city and put the speedometer needle in the red. Within a half hour, the last few commuters waved goodbye, and we set off for the unspoiled Black Sea mountain range surrounding the city.

The monastery, like a natural growth, clung to the side of a sheer cliff near the top. Built in the fourth century by Greek Orthodox monks, the retreat had offered a sanctuary deep in the wilderness from worldly temptation. The area remained pristine late in the twentieth century. Except for the two-lane blacktop far below Sumela, little had changed.

Starting up the steep, narrow path crowded by evergreens on both sides, we encountered no pilgrims, tourists, or guards. While entering like Dante the dark wood, I heard a distinct warbling from the shrubbery. "What's that birdsong?" I wondered. "Those are nightingales,"

Andrew replied. I stopped to listen for a few seconds. "I thought they only sang at night," I protested. "No," he answered, "they call during the day, especially in late afternoon and at dusk."

Next to the death of Bambi's mother, the *bulbul* warbling proved the biggest disappointment of my life. I quickly realized that unlike the Keats persona, I was not transported. Darkly I listened, but did not utter *"Komm Susser Tod."* I resolved to live several more decades before succumbing to the avian siren song: *descensus Averno* remained on indefinite hold. "Well, I have been reading about the dulcet sounds of Paradise, a staple trope in all national literatures, but I have never heard the off-key chirping until now. The literary imagination triumphs over the empirical facts every time." My friend laughed. "That's why I study history," he said. "Documents can be verified and dated."

I had also read some historical accounts, such as northern and southern versions of the War of the Rebellion. "Yeah, as you know better than I, fiction is not confined to novels. Take the case of Jefferson, who is enshrined on Mt. Rushmore. For two hundred years, top scholars denied that he raped his servant and sired illegitimate, mulatto children, which he never acknowledged. Guess what? Guilty as charged. DNA samples don't lie." Andrew, who had quickened his pace, made no reply.

Trudging up the ever-steeper path, I passed the tree line and found myself standing at the base of the cliff, a sublime moment. The monastery, high above, beckoned like a precious talisman. I held no brief for theological doctrine, but I recalled the philosophical masterwork by William James, *Varieties of Religious Experience.* I felt, momentarily, as one with the pilgrims who had set off by ship from the Greek islands some two thousand years before, braving the elements, pirates, and hostile tribes in foreign countries. After months, perhaps years, the night sea journey had brought the sojourners to their goal, which had glowed softly in the waning light from the rock face like the Grail: a sense of peace that had surpassed understanding.

"Hey, Andrew," I shouted. "Hold up a minute; I'm catching my breath." Joining him at wide turn that offered a million-dollar view of the West canyon, I repeated an old joke. "A tightrope walker and a guy getting a blow job from an eighty-year-old woman have the same thought: 'Don't look down.' " Andrew chuckled politely and pointed straight up. "Steady on, mate. We should reach the entrance well before dark. No artificial lighting up here, you know. I want to take pictures of the murals inside the monastery."

Yet, the hand-painted images of Christian saints high on the chapel walls had been effectively ruined. According to the tenets of Islam, the sacred could not be represented except in writing. Arabic script, of course, was highly elaborate and aesthetically pleasing, but did not depict the human image. At some point in history, after the monks had withdrawn and Mohammed's faithful had occupied Anatolia with Constantinople the center of the Caliphate, cathedrals had become mosques and Christian monasteries had been abandoned and defaced for the greater glory of Allah.

The interior consisted of several large, high-ceilinged rooms vacant of furnishings; stones, chunks of plaster, twigs, and non-descript trash littered the floor. After a moment of contemplation, we exchanged disappointed glances. "Let's get back to town before last light," Andrew suggested, and we made our way down the steep pathway to the waiting van. Andrew and I occupied the rear wide seat, leaned back comfortably, and relaxed for the long ride to the hotel. A few kilometers down a steep hill, the driver slowed and pulled over to the side. A group of sheepherders led by a tall, bearded man carrying a biblical staff had waved us down. Andrew leaned forward to unlock the right cargo door and within a few seconds, all forward seats had been taken. None of the passengers greeted us or glanced in our direction.

Minutes later, the van veered to the right and crossed a narrow wooden bridge, the flimsy handrails barely clearing the sides. A wide gravel path, heavily pocked with washed-out patches that did not qualify as a road, led at a steep grade up the mountainside. No guardrails, much less room for oncoming vehicles, animals, or pedestrians. I glanced out my window and calculated that the left wheels rested dangerously close to the edge. At the base of the incline, our intrepid driver came to a full stop. He passed cigarettes to the shepherds, and when everyone lit up and inhaled deeply, he shifted into low gear, gunned the powerful engine, and put the hammer down.

As a teenager, heedless of oblivion, I had given certain disaster short shrift by driving 100 mph in badly maintained cars and oversized motorcycles; I had braved the Palisades Park Ferris wheel and the Coney Island dragon coaster. By fifty-three and counting, however, I preferred safe vehicles that observed the speed limit. Motorcycles did not tempt me, and I took a pass on theme parks, with their death-defying thrill rides. Despite my precautions, I was unexpectedly riding, third class, the Doomsday Express. Part way up the Turkish mountainside, all four wheels skidding, engine straining, rocks bouncing off the chassis, I looked straight down at what would surely be the following day's headlines: "Van Plunges into Ravine; No Survivors." As a sympathetic maneuver, I shifted to the right until I invaded Andrew's lap. Distantly, I heard someone in a British accent say, "Are you all right?"—which question felt like a rude awakening. "Yeah," I muttered and regained my composure.

Reaching the summit, the passengers thanked the driver and headed for green pastures. Our pilot then expertly turned left on the short abutment, backed a few feet, wrenched the wheel sharply to the left again, and headed to the paved road below—a respite from the adrenaline high and a return to normal blood pressure. My entire life had not flashed before me, as often reported by those who had survived a near-death experience, but I had felt less anxiety on the Cessna 180 strut before my first static-line jump at 2,000 feet.

. . . .

Two days later, safe in the faculty lounge, a colleague said, "I heard that you and Andrew checked out the Sumela Monastery. Was it worth the long bus trip to Trabzon?" I had a ready answer, "Yeah, man, it's to die for."

XII.

The Gladstone Connection[2]

And remember, no matter where you go, there you are.
— Confucious

Following a tour of Cappadocia's underground city in Anatolia, Turkey, Jeff Hickson and I took a bus trip southeast—a hazardous, uncomfortable journey—to an unpronounceable coastal town in Hatay province, once part of neighboring Syria. My command of Turkish was virtually nil, but I spoke some Arabic, and owing to vicissitudes of history, the population was bilingual. At the bus stop, a personable young man offered well-appointed, separate rooms at a reasonable price. After spits of kebab loaded on pita bread and obligatory rounds of *ouzo*, we slumbered like the Ephesus Seven for ten hours straight. The next morning we awoke refreshed, hungry for pistachios and lamb; pockets bulging with Turkish lira, we headed for the coastal quarter famous for eateries, rug shops, and leather goods.

We were not disappointed, though toward the end of the meal, street urchins brazenly grabbed Jeff's wallet/passport off the table and scampered down a narrow alley. Luckily, the thieves were soon apprehended by observant, polyglot touts, who chased down pre-adolescent scoundrels that patrolled the area—for *baksheesh*, not (literally) a tip as most people think, but a "gift."

Barely fifty feet from dining *al fresco*, we were ushered into The Oriental Rug Emporium by a strapping lad wearing a suede windbreaker, a living manikin for clothing and accessories. By coincidence, his uncle owned a nearby leather shop, offering a wide

[2] October 2014 *Curitiba in English*, edit. Michael Rubin

selection of jackets, overcoats, gloves, and boots. But first we were invited to admire the tribal/city rugs rolled and stacked high against three walls of the spacious showroom. The merchandise gave off a musty aroma that, when combined with incense, human sweat, and teakettle smells, produced a unique *eau de cologne à la Türkiye*.

Prominently displayed on a large wooden frame, the emporium masterpiece: a Persian city carpet with a complex design of vibrant colors, each separate flora and fauna magnetized by the Tree of Life at the center. The woven figures produced a three-dimensional effect, so delicate and well executed that I failed to notice the deliberate flaw, since Allah alone was perfect.

A squat, graying man stood at the entrance, beaming and arms extended. "*Ahlan wa sahlan!*" he exclaimed. "*Sabah al-khair,*" I replied. He blinked. "*Sabah al-noor,*" he answered. "Do you speak Arabic?" I hesitated before saying, "Just a few words. I studied in Riyadh and Tunis." He look pleased. "Well, my friend, we can do business as brothers." I pointed to the rug on display. "How much for that piece?" I asked, expecting a boxcar number. "Well, *habibi*, we don't sell carpets like apples. Come, *nashrub chai*. You haven't even counted the knots," he added. "Just asking," I said, turning and stepping into the street, freshened by the sea breeze.

Once on the sidewalk, we headed toward the Mediterranean. "What's the hurry?" Jeff asked. "We have all day, and the rugs looked fine. We might have gotten a good price." I quickened the pace, answering, "You don't know these guys. After a few cups of apple tea, they turn on the charm and the high pressure. They'll literally twist your arm to keep you in the store. I know their tricks. I might be *touring* in a country village, but I wasn't *born* here." At the corner, I heard quick steps and loud breathing.

It was the rug merchant, glaring, lips white with fury. We made horrible eye contact. "You know nothing about rugs!" he announced and stalked away angrily. I chuckled. "What's so funny?" my friend wondered. "He thinks I'm the competition, sent to check prices," I answered. "I am flattered, but ironically he's right. I know next to nothing about rugs."

Suddenly, a childhood flashback took form in a simultaneously strange-familiar travel bag in a leather shop window. Among various luggage pieces, motorcycle jackets, suede winter coats, and riding boots squatted a Gladstone of faded memory. I'd never seen the genuine article except in certain pre-midcentury black and white movies, a well-established genre of the era. The film script had been predictably formulaic: a forbidden love story complicated by a subplot, typically Axis-power espionage, imminent financial catastrophe, and unintended felony—the usual Hollywood contrivances. The narrative had followed strict conventions of the period, specifically, the inciting moment when the heroine, despite her Puritanical inhibitions and feeble resistance, had engaged in a passionate embrace, her full lips parted in submission. Unable to appreciate fully the sexual implications of adult love scenes, I had simply endured the kissing close-ups with a measure of disdain.

In the pre-air-travel era, another *de rigueur* scene had engaged my full attention: the train station departure. There the scenario had played out with little variation: a party of two arrived at the crowded depot with minutes to spare. The dialogue between the unmarried couple was brief, intense. The engine, like a medieval dragon, hissed impatiently, building steam for the long trip west: exotic, romantic, fraught with unnamed peril and mystery. The suave leading man with a buried past wore an expensive overcoat and fedora. He carried a Gladstone bag, bulging but firmly strapped, with a brass locking mechanism and studded with rivets.

No exceptions—always the same luggage—which had served both as carryall and metonymy: adventure, independence, and unexplored territory both objective and psychological in scope. Once the train had cleared Grand Central Station, picking up steam, white smoke belching from the stack, anything would have been possible: an uninhibited, passionate woman in the dining car boldly asking for a light; the dark-skinned stranger with a cruel facial scar who shared the first class compartment; a high-stakes card game with a marked deck; or a late-night inspection by uniformed authorities—no end to the unexpected on the Midnight Express.

I am not impulsive. I learned in the Orient that patience is a virtue. But as Bob Newhart had conceded after an earnest waiter had described a luscious ice cream sundae in mouth-watering detail, "I'm not made of stone." Although separated by the glass show window, not to mention several million lira, the bag was already mine! I turned to Jeff, who gazed at a pebbled leather briefcase. "Hey, man, loan me your stash—just in case this pirate out-bargains me, and I'll repay you, as Chekhov put it, 'in the other world.'"

My friend complied, and haggling phrases at the ready, I entered briskly, nearly colliding with the owner, who had been about to pull me by the arm into his dark, leathery enclave. On that occasion, I didn't negotiate the price, although I had had sufficient practice at the hajj carpet *souq* in Saudi Arabia years before. Upon entry, the proprietor locked the door, rendering me a virtual (willing) prisoner and leaving my friend alone and friendless outside. Soon, we came to a satisfactory agreement: a quick sale at an inflated price for the merchant, an unexpected nostalgic embrace for me in prime middle age.

Kierkegaard cautioned against a fixation on privileged moments, and Sartre argued in *Nausée* that perfect moments (his variation on the term), which were magical, didn't exist, since the material world did not accommodate a perfect set of circumstances. I beg to differ. The magic *does* occur in emotionally bound memories, and I had joined my childhood fantasy with empirical reality for a reasonable sum. I had made a financial/psychological bargain, the fabled once-in-a-lifetime event. Triumphant, like a Roman gladiator after victory, I exited the shop with my genuine Gladstone to greet the envious world.

For the following twenty-five years, I explored three continents, a dozen countries, and scores of cities. I walked, hitchhiked, and used all forms of public transportation including trolley, rickshaw, and shuttle. In Jordan, I entered the Nabataean ruins on horseback.

Regardless, I traveled light: the Gladstone—faded, scratched, scraped—served me well, until last month, when I noticed the metal clasp had mysteriously disappeared. The leather straps functioned, but the bag was ruined aesthetically, if not functionally, beyond repair. I didn't hesitate. Searching web sites, I soon located another genuine Gladstone to replace the battered Turkish travel bag. It's a handmade piece by a British Columbia firm for a mere 950 CA, which converts to $857.72 USD. Far beyond the original price I had gladly paid in Turkey, but according to the color photograph, the bag was well worth the fee in craftsmanship, appearance, and quality. Each piece is custom built, so I now must wait while the leathersmith builds the piece to specifications.

When the treasure arrives, I will make a dry run to test its efficacy, for Hegel observed that function alone confirms reality. Consequently, a handmade Gladstone unused is not, in the philosophical sense, genuine luggage but a beautiful object for admiration and no more. I am aging fast; close companions/family members whom I had cherished since childhood are gone. My academic career is long over; exotic adventures are no longer likely. Yet it's "not too late to seek a newer world," as Tennyson observed. In fact, the childhood film *noir* luggage made manifest determines renewed interest in jet/cruise brochures. I note that, except for a short stay in Cancun, my passport lacks stamps south of the border. Costa Rica, Puerto Rico, and Bermuda all beckon. As a latter day knight-errant, I require a personal calling card imprinted: "Paladin. Have Gladstone, Must Travel."

XIII.

On the Road to Damascus

A journey is a fragment of Hell.—Koran

My friend-colleague Moodie Hourani and I, while heading for the Ankara bus station during Christmas break one misty morning well before dawn in 1991, broke off our conversation when the cab's headlights illuminated a large grey owl on the south Bilkent campus road. We exchanged glances. In cultural symbolism, the owl could mean wisdom or a harbinger of death. Hegel famously suggested that Minerva's totem bird, which only flies at night, augurs a new philosophical era. An omen of good or bad fortune? Either option, though radically different, seemed quite possible. Travel, according to the commonplace observation, enlarges the mind, and some well-worn clichés, like that one, are true.

Nevertheless, travel throughout the Middle East, as recorded by Halliburton, Stark, Thesinger, Theroux, Lawrence, and many other intrepid adventurers east of the Suez, often includes mortal danger, ranging from ill luck to late twentieth-century terrorism, from exotic diseases to kidnapping and murder. For "rich" English-speaking tourists, counterfeit artifacts, bogus site-seeing tours, inflated exchange rates, and outright theft are not unknown. Yet as an old hand, I put anxiety aside and chose the better option: wisdom. As for the creature of the night, the owl spread its massive wings, and soon airborne, disappeared into the morning mist.

Moodie leaned forward and spoke briefly to the driver in Turkish. The rich odor of tobacco hung like artificial fog in the taxi, all windows tightly shut. Arriving safely in downtown Ankara, I tipped the driver handsomely while Moodie surveyed the swarming streets of downtown Ankara. He turned to me and said that since we were still early, we could stop for coffee only two blocks from the station. I concurred.

Overseas, I often traveled alone; on that occasion I reflected on the fact that my companion would provide not only good conversation but the perks of an expert guide: fluency in Arabic and firsthand knowledge of Damascus (where, though born of Palestinian parents in Wales, he had spent his early childhood). Dr. Hourani spoke impeccable British English with a posh accent, complementing the manners of a Victorian gentleman. He had suggested the Damascus junket like a formal invitation: "Cliff, our colleague Professor Hamburg (in fact, his American girlfriend, Claire) declined to join me for the holiday. Would you like to accompany me instead?" I had immediately agreed to his suggestion: a welcome break from campus life, an opportunity to practice Arabic with a safety net, and travel, along with the inevitable adventures, for its own sake.

After a cup of bitter Turkish coffee at a nearby café, we reached the bus station in good time for departure. The crowded terminal reeked of sweat, dust, tobacco fumes, and sewage emanating from the toilet, doorless and gaping like the entrance to the underworld. Standing in line, our travel companions made enquiries, the usual practice in the xenophobic Middle East, though (other factors being equal) English speaking citizens were generally addressed in polite tones.

Suddenly, a young man with dark stubble and a bleary countenance jumped the queue. No one affected to notice. He carried a white canvas bag crammed with heterogeneous goods: a petty smuggler. Mehmet, after a brief introduction, explained the operation. He bought cheap toys, watches, and risqué postcards in Turkey, selling them at a profit in Damascus. On the return trip, he carried hand-carved chess sets, checkerboards, paintings on velvet, and the usual kitsch. He sold the items to Ankara shops that catered to the tourist trade. With the profits, he made monthly payments on a small, picturesque cottage located near the Mediterranean coast. Anxious to share in his good fortune, Mehmet eagerly provided monochromatic photos of his future retirement home, now abandoned and boarded like a haunted house. The weather-beaten old building resembled a tinderbox ready to blaze like a meteor at the drop of a lit cigarette.

After boarding the crowded coach, the air already polluted by tobacco smoke, I mentally converted the ticket price from Turkish lira into American currency. A round-trip from Ankara to Damascus cost $3.50 USD, a bargain for the two-day journey. However, nothing that cheap was exactly free of peril. In fact, you might not have made it. Fueled by a powerful caffeine-saturated potion, the exhausted bus driver, muttering prayers, sped recklessly both ways in order to earn enough for the next journey, followed by a brief rest, then another—and so on, *ad nauseam*, or more likely, *ad infinitum*. Allah is merciful, compassionate—but calculates the odds.

Soon after everyone was seated, chatting amiably with his neighbor, and we were on our way—the vehicle backfiring and belching black smoke like a volcano. As we headed toward the mountain range, I was reminded of Siddhartha as a young merchant, who had traveled to conduct business in another village. The arrangement, from a financial standpoint, had proved a failure. Still, he had savored every moment, the Zen melding of being and time: Be-Here-Now. The journey, the people, the food, the weather—all contributing to a sense of stasis, pure enjoyment. Having renounced the goal, the youthful Bodhisattva had merged with his surroundings and absorbed the gratification of the senses by cherishing the simplest activities and appreciating fully the treasure of existence itself and not mindful of artificial purpose.

Actually, I hated every minute of the journey to Damascus—truly a fragment of hell from beginning to end. The cheap bus tickets no longer mattered, for the price did not balance the misery. My primary senses were attacked by thick tobacco smoke, whining engine, grinding gears, and foul human odors, all while being constantly jolted on the torn, unpadded seat over bad roads through narrow mountain passes—the abominable cacophony assaulted mind, body, and spirit. Though I dozed fitfully out of sheer boredom during the dark passage, my head sometimes striking the cold window, a restful sleep proved impossible. I dreamt of stormy moors with earth tremors. While groggily awake, civil conversation proved out of the question. Owing to the motor's steady drone, the violent swerves as the driver expertly negotiated hairpin turns and passed semi-trailers on the steep hills, the asphyxiating fumes reducing each utterance to gasps punctuated by stammer; thus, the pragmatics of discourse was defeated by the Byzantine yoke.

After a long day's journey into night, we arrived in Antochia early the next afternoon. Creakily, we debussed. I took the luggage while Moodie made arrangements to cross the frontier. We agreed to meet at a nearby hotel coffee shop in about an hour. To the right of the entrance, I placed our bags under the nearest table for safe keeping and waited for service. Unexpectedly, I heard snatches of conversation in Arabic, as opposed to Turkish, and noticed two young men seated at either end of a bench, with a substantial loaf between them. Muttering happily, each tore small pieces of crust and dipped the morsel into one of several knife cuts oozing dark gravy. They exchanged terms of enjoyment: *quais* [good], *jamil* [beautiful], and *momtaz* [excellent] between bites. When the server approached, one of the stalwarts exclaimed, *"Garsoon, atini ithnan bebsee, barida* [Waiter, bring me two cold Pepsis]." I then remembered from a previous trip to eastern Turkey that the biblical Antioch, once part of Syria, was bi-lingual. I had memorized little Turkish, and my pidgin Arabic was rusty, but still adequate to order *shai bedun sucre.*

Moodie arrived with the itinerary. We would take a taxi to the frontier and board the bus to Hams. The following morning we would make arrangements for the short trip into Damascus. Once there, we would book a room at the Hotel *al-Famia,* which had been recommended by a well-traveled colleague.

After a painful bus ride from Ankara, we were nearly there, spared the usual bureaucratic delays or commonplace travel mishaps. In possession of vacation money in two currencies, valid passports, and luggage, we were prepared to raid the sprawling *Al-Hamidiyah Souq,* a bargain-hunter's paradise.

2.

Damascus, like Cairo, predates the spread of Islam. After the Muslim conquest in the seventh century, a metropolitan trading center had assumed the standard Middle Eastern pattern: *mosque, madrassa, souq*. Those institutions had corresponded to the basics of existence in that prayer, education, and material goods had offered spiritual, intellectual, and physical comfort to believers who populated/administered the city and, often, the country at large. Thus, in the shadow of the great mosque, *Al-Hamidiyah Souq*, with its labyrinthine pathways, provided an endless bounty of foodstuffs, clothing, furniture, toys, games, rugs, weaponry, souvenirs, and much else for locals and tourists alike. A casual stroll through the seemingly endless maze of small shops and stalls might take several hours. No one was ever lost, however, since the *Umayyad* mosque, like the pole star, oriented the sojourner at a glance.

Well prepared with Syrian pounds and Arabic bargaining techniques, Moodie and I crossed the street near the central post office and began our journey into the heart of the Damascus bazaar. The shop owners were delighted to welcome our custom. The first Gulf War, combined with an unusually harsh winter compounded by Byzantine intrigues shrouded in secrecy according to the established practice of dictators, had virtually eliminated tourism in 1991. Moodie and I had the bounty to ourselves. Always on the lookout for trade, men and boys shouted, "*Salaam. Apfel chai, saddeeqi* [Peace. Apple tea, my friend]." in narrow doorways or behind large tables loaded with a variety of goods, both manufactured and handmade.

Partway down a dark alley smelling of fresh bread, flowers, slightly spoiled fruit, and incense, Moodie gestured to an entrance partly blocked by a middle-aged man positively glowing with goodwill toward a possible windfall, likely his first sale in days, and our new-found friend welcomed the opportunity to fleece a couple of infidels. Nevertheless, I appreciated the enthusiastic welcome—even if I didn't quite believe clichés of hospitality.

Inside the cluttered store, we engaged in the well-worn routine. English might be the language of diplomacy, but Arabic was the *lingua franca* of bargaining. Yet our portly host, whose large, steaming teapot resembled an artifact out of *One Thousand and One Nights*, soon realized that he had miscalculated in a major respect: I spoke some merchant Arabic, and Moodie was fluent in the language, which was not only grammatically complicated—even for native speakers—but also compellingly beautiful in each of its several dialects. The first few words established both identity and pecking order by virtue of idiom, tone, and accent.

Thus, Mohammed revealed by his musical delivery that he had emigrated from nearby Lebanon to set up shop, quite literally, in Damascus. Moodie's expression proved more difficult to identify. Although he had been reared shortly after birth in Damascus, he had also spent several years in Palestine, home of his ancestors, and Saudi Arabia, where he taught linguistics to young scholars of various nationalities ranging from Yemen to Africa, from Jordan to Iraq. I spoke, haltingly, the Najdi dialect, clearly a Western novice and a late starter in studying the classical language. Since we all three shared English and Arabic, albeit unevenly, we engaged in smalltalk over apple tea before the bargaining ritual began.

"And what can I offer you, my friends?" Mohammed asked, smooth as the Turkish green honey (the world's best) that glowed from jars on the lower shelf. "I have everything: hand-carved chess, antique weapons used during the Crusades, hand-stitched tablecloths in four colors. The best, *habibi*, nothing but the best."

I gazed at the clutter of goods on tables of various sizes and wide shelves from floor to ceiling. "How much for a chess set?" I asked. "Please! Let us not speak of money. Is money so important? Wait one moment; help yourself to my poor refreshments. I'll return soon."

Mohammed rose majestically, swept out of the main display area, and disappeared into the back room. Soon he returned with several checkerboards and cotton sacks of chess pieces, which he emptied to produce a small pile near each board. He spread his wares on a city carpet with an intricate design representing the Persian paradise.

"Now," he said quietly, "you can see that these items are not of the same quality. Which do you choose?" I pointed to the set on the far left. The shop owner approved. "You have excellent taste. I see that you have identified the finest craftsmanship, the best of the lot."

"And the price?" I asked evenly. "In American dollars, what will you give a poor man?" he replied. "Three dollars," I said firmly. He chuckled like a drain. "I sold a set, its twin in quality, for $80.00 just this morning. I swear to the God!"

"Five dollars on the black market will stuff a pillow case in your currency," I countered. Mohammed sighed, "And my precious bride, who perhaps will bless me with a boy once again, must starve in these unfortunate times. Twenty-five dollars will allow me to open my doors tomorrow, *inshallah*."

"All right, eight dollars plus all the silver in my leather purse and no more." Mohammed said, "I cannot make a profit, but I know my tablecloths will prove irresistible, so I will agree." He collected the chess pieces, dropped them into the sack, and drew the string tight. He placed the item near the cash box. I counted out the bills and change from my purse, which added up to $1.33. "But wait!" he cried with a stricken expression. "You haven't yet seen my tablecloths. Just one moment."

I glanced at Moodie, who watched the proceedings with amused interest, and he indicated assent. He then rose, turned toward the door, and said, "I'll return in twenty minutes' time." A moment later, as promised, Mohammed made his grand entrance with seven or eight folded tablecloths, the top item gently cupping his chin.

Seated, legs crossed, we made offers and counter offers; we told anecdotes about Middle Eastern travel; we argued fine points of quality; we pretended to conclude the proceedings; and eventually, predictably, we came to an agreement. I bought four hand-stitched tablecloths, including eight matching napkins for each item, with one full set gratis. After the hard bargaining on a hard, cold floor and several additional bladder-busting glasses of tea, I paid eighteen dollars per unit.

Moodie returned with a large, circular package, wrapped in brown butcher paper. "I bought homemade sweets for my staff back in Turkey," he explained. "They deserve it; I drove them hard last term." My friend and the shop owner then glared at one another like two bulls during the rutting season. Another half hour passed while Moodie and Mohammed, like tribal enemies, haggled in Arabic faster than I could understand over pajamas, a prayer rug, several posters featuring a warrior *bedu* in full cry, and silver earrings, along with a half dozen top-quality tablecloths. Finally, loaded like Oriental merchants of the Silk Road, we moved toward the exit. "*Shokran katheer; ma'salaama; hyakallah, habibi.*"

Moving briskly, Mohammed literally blocked the door with his wide hips. "But wait, *ya akhi,*" he said, making eye contact like a hypnotist. "Come with me, and I will show you something rare." I had lived in the Middle East long enough to know that one cannot avoid fate. Leaving my friend to stand guard over our purchases, I followed the owner up a narrow stairway located at the back of the emporium. In the dark, narrow attic, he pulled a cord to light the area in a yellowish hue, casting shadows on the wall.

Reaching for a metal scabbard hanging from a hook, Mohammed handed me a small *khanjar,* the Arabian hooked dagger of Oriental history and folklore. Uncannily, Mohammed had guessed that I, and not my Arabic speaking friend, held a fascination for edged weapons. From early childhood I had bought, traded, and lost several folders, switchblades, and straight-edge knives, including expensive custom pieces by top US craftsmen. I already owned a tanto, a *kukri,* and a hand made butterfly knife, but I was missing and lusting for a *khanjar* with its wicked curved blade. In fact, I had resolved to purchase a traditional Yemeni dagger before leaving Damascus, but had planned to arrange that purchase later, after carefully checking quality and price in various shops throughout the bazaar.

I turned the object in my hand, admiring the smooth goat-bone handle. Drawing the steel, I noticed an inscription in Kufic, which Mohammed translated: "Hurl thy thunderbolt." The double-edged blade was honed like a razor; the tip came to a needle point, thirsting for an infidel's jugular. In sympathy with the blade's contour, I was hooked. "Very old," the manager said solemnly. I knew better, of course, but the dagger did look authentic. "*Becom?*" I asked. "*Myatt arba,*" he stated firmly. "Not four hundred dollars!" I exclaimed. He replied quietly: "*Nam.*"

Time passed, and my bladder ached. "*Hamam* [bathroom]?" I gasped. "*Maffee* [not in]," he replied, suppressing a smile. The bargaining continued for another three rounds, but we remained far apart. Desperate, I produced a twenty-dollar bill. "Take it, and go in peace," I said sternly. He stared at the engraved picture of Stonewall Jackson and pulled it gently out of my grasp. "I lose," he sobbed. "But I need the money."

I trotted down the rickety stairs in triumph and agony, the generous supply of tea demanding release. "Moodie," I shouted, "where's the nearest bathroom?" "Make a left, and go to the basement of the rug shop on the corner," he answered. "Give the old boy a tip on the way out."

After a long pause at the foul-smelling urinal, I handed the attendant a handsome gift in Syrian pounds. Later, while passing the Great Mosque and heading for the post office, Moodie asked the standard question: "How much did you finally pay for the dagger?" "Twenty bucks," I replied. "About sixteen quid," Moodie culculated. "He robbed you. I could have gotten it for you much cheaper." Like vaudeville characters, we all played our roles and repeated the well-rehearsed lines. Travel through the Middle East was a "literary" event, intertextual.

The trip back to Ankara should have been a matter of buying a ticket, boarding the bus, and simple survival until we arrived at the capital, tired but alive and well. The return journey, however, was not entirely smooth sailing, beginning with the bus tickets, which were sold at the post office. While waiting in line, an official intervened on our behalf and invited us into his private office, sparsely furnished and unheated, for a glass of tea. He spoke passable English and enquired with great interest about my background in the States ("Are you from Ohio?") and our candid opinion of the Turks, who were not held in high esteem east of Antochia, which rightfully belonged to Syria. He was most accommodating and friendly; he offered suggestions; he proffered disinformation—in the Oriental fashion. Thus, we missed the morning bus to Turkey by at least an hour, which meant a long taxi ride to the shipping depot, where we spent part of the day mailing our precious goods designated for family and friends abroad.

The large shipping room was filled with people of various nationalities filling out forms, addressing boxes, and arguing about the procedure. Long fingers of cigarette smoke hung in the air, which smelled like an old tobacco shed and dirty laundry. I approached the counter, and before I could form a sentence, a tall man with thick glasses handed me several flat sheets of cardboard, which could be assembled into boxes, and lengths of thick twine, cutting the ties with a crescent-moon finger-knife. He pointed to a pile of forms, marked in thick Arabic numerals, which I counted as I collected two copies each. A squat vase held felt-tip pens in various colors. I then reached for my wallet with an inquisitive expression. The counterman shook his head, and I understood that the charge for those items would be added to the shipping cost.

Carrying the cardboard, I made my way through the busy packers until I found Moodie sorting our loot into separate piles. We soon set to work loading and tying boxes. That small chore accomplished, we discovered that neither of us could read the forms, written in an official and unfamiliar vocabulary. Fellow patrons looked equally baffled or unwilling to help. My head was spinning from the foul odors, my patience exhausted. I accepted defeat. We would lug our goods across town, load them in the cargo hold of the bus, and take them across the frontier.

Like the *deus ex machina*, a friendly young clerk appeared unexpectedly, and speaking flawless English, he answered our questions and solved the technical problems in a prompt, efficient manner. While we attended to the packing detail, he filled out the forms, asking questions when necessary. In a few minutes, I exclaimed, *"Khalas!"*, using the Saudi idiom for "finished." I then turned to the helpful young man with a fistful of currency, several pounds over the amount for the materials and postage. "That's not necessary," he said, smiling. "But tea money is," I answered. "And *Allah kareem* [God is generous]."

Stuffing the money in his shirt pocket without bothering to count it, our assistant pointed toward a dark hallway to the right of the counter. "Add your cartons to the pile over there," he said and walked away. After dragging the boxes to a railway wagon stacked high with containers like our own, we were left with only two shopping bags, plus our luggage at the hotel, with most of the *souq* treasures tagged for home. We had scheduled a later departure, but assuming the gifts would arrive in good order, the delay had proved fortuitous. In that instance, and not for the first or last time, error coincided with serendipity, like in a clumsy Hollywood script. "What next?" I asked. "We still have a couple of hours before the bus leaves."

Moodie looked thoughtful. "Right," he said, "we can have a leisurely dinner. I know a good restaurant just outside the city. After eating, we'll pick up our bags, check out, and take a cab to the bus station. We will be a bit early, mind, but you never know."

Exactly. Our bus tickets did not match the new schedule. A simple exchange would have solved the problem, but the discrepancy caused a minor uproar. Two transportation personnel, one in a uniform with medals, shouted at each other. We were asked to produce our passports and proof of solvency—at least forty dollars in hard currency.

When the manager checked Moodie's identification, his demeanor changed. "Hourani," he intoned. "Is Abdullah *aljooz* (old man) your relative?" Moodie leaned forward, saying, "He is my grandfather. I lived with him in *Al Wizarat* during the first years of the Israeli Occupation." The official pronounced, "In that case, we can resolve this minor issue," he assured us. He motioned to the younger clerk, who punched our tickets and handed the holy relics to Moodie and me with a polite expression in Arabic.

At twilight, with our luggage in the hold and shopping bags under the seats, we headed west to Antochia. An attendant served cold soda and a bulging napkin of almonds, the best I ever tasted. The roads were good, and I nodded off. . .until we suddenly veered to the right and stopped short with a hiss of air brakes. The rear doors flew open, and two young men threw several burlap bags into the aisle before climbing aboard. I locked eyes with the first young man who wore a traditional *thobe* with a heavy cape and moved quickly to stack the bags. "Is this legal?" I asked. "Illegal!" he answered promptly. I took hold of the top bundle, bulging with contraband, and shoved it under an empty seat in the penultimate row. The second smuggler, wearing Western clothes and a thick mustache that hid his mouth, muttered, "*Yella* [Get out of the way]." I turned toward him angrily, saying, "*Shuway shuway, habibi* [Slow down, buddy]!" He said nothing, but glowered as he moved the remaining sacks to clear the aisle. No one else took notice of the unexpected stop, adding cargo and passengers with no tickets to ride.

The first smuggler smiled, showing white, even teeth. He expressed a friendly, yet slightly formal demeanor, setting me at ease. "You speak the Arabic language?" he enquired. "A little. I lived in Saudi for three years." He extended his hand. "Good, but you told Abdullah to *speak* more slowly before. My name is Nasser, but I'm not Egyptian. From the West Bank. Since five years old, I lived in Kuwait. I worked for an international shipping firm. . .until we got kicked out." I shook my head, answering, "Yeah, Arafat backed the wrong horse." Nasser laughed in agreement.

"We will reach the border by dawn, and I must sleep. Good night," he said in a Arabic. "And you are among those people," I replied, using the standard phrase. I returned to my seat. Moodie had dozed off as we continued our journey. For a few minutes, I attempted to recall the Arabic expression for "calm down," but failed. I drifted off to sleep and dreamt of my younger brother, a musician, who, when asked if he knew "Sheik, Sheik, Shariq," had replied, "Know it! I wrote it." Too soon for a good rest, the bus slowed, and the attendant switched on the lights, burning my eyes. "Looks like we are at the border," I mumbled and stretched painfully.

At the driver's command, we emptied the coach, most carrying shopping bags into the cold morning. Moodie asked the driver for directions to the men's room, while the passengers sat uncomfortably on a concrete curb. Syrian and Turkish soldiers searched the vehicle, which had pulled fifty yards ahead, for contraband. I looked anxiously at Nasser, smoking a *bidi*, who understood my concern. "No problem," he pronounced, "they will take the money." Alone, neither smuggler kept shopping bags nearby; their illegal goods—soap, towels, razors, baby diapers, etc.—remained hidden in plain sight aboard the coach.

Although bribes were often reliable, it was still risky business. A bust meant prison and no mistake. Those who served time (and not everyone survived) aged quickly, and a prison record, like a tattoo, was forever. Moreover, the smugglers were already marked men. By the judgment of social history, Palestinians were generally held in contempt by their fellow Muslims on the principle that no people worth respect would consent to Israeli occupation. The argument was specious, of course, but Western logic did not necessarily determine justice in the Middle East.

To ease the tension, we engaged in conversation. "I lived with my family in Kuwait since the nineteen seventies," Nasser said sadly. "I had a good job, and my wife gave me four sons, *al-ḥamdulillah*. Then the Americans invaded, and after the ceasefire, the king made all the Palestinians leave. I can't go back to Ramallah now. This," he said, glancing at the bus, "is my fate."

Not to be outdone, I replied with a similar story, though not entirely true, at least in terms of the tragic implications. "I taught in the States for almost twenty years and lost my job. I finally signed a contract overseas, but I did not take my family. I haven't seen my son in more than ten years. When I retire, I have no place to live." Nasser glanced at Abdullah and then turned to me. "This is the life," he said solemnly in his native tongue. "What can we do?" I replied rhetorically. Abdullah, who had not spoken a word of English thus far, exclaimed, "Nothing!" Understood. We three world travelers, awaiting our fate at the Turkish frontier, reflected on our lot.

A border guard approached and motioned to inspect my bags. After a cursory glance at the items, he seemed nonplused: a traditional dagger, tablecloths, chess sets, all standard souvenirs from Damascus caused no concern. The officer and I exchanged departure phrases, and he moved toward the couple on the right, whose purchases looked more interesting. A moment later, our bus pulled up to a large building, where the passengers were directed inside for the exit formalities.

Once assembled outside the main office, a security officer emerged and shouted, "*Jawazee!*" I had learned the meaning of that phrase upon arriving in Saudi Arabia in 1980: "Give me your passport." Moments later an official called out names/nationalities and returned each item to its rightful owner. The married men provided the service for their wives, who waited in the bus. Everyone inspected his freshly stamped document but Moodie, who remained empty-handed. Without a passport, one was stranded, a secular limbo equally painful, but with fewer prospects for salvation. I looked anxiously for an explanation. We were about to cross into Turkey. From inside the office, someone shouted, "*Englizi!*" Moodie entered, and the assistant closed the door. I waited several minutes and entered the official sanctuary after a light knock.

Moodie stood before the large wooden desk, his head hanging like a delinquent schoolboy. "What's going on?" I demanded. The official busy filling out a form ignored my question. "I have to pay an exit fee," my friend said quietly. "Ten pounds Sterling." As a matter of policy, I had never bribed officials, which though a common practice in some counties, remained against the law. But exceptions occur. "Hell, I'll put up any amount," I said staring at the manager, who glanced up and shook his head slowly from side to side. "No, I have to wait until the bank opens at 9:00," Moodie explained. "He will only accept a ten-pound note in English currency."

I muttered something unprintable, adding, "All right, then, I'll go with the luggage across the border and wait for you at the shelter in Antochia." Moodie agreed, and I headed for the door. But the frontier hassle was not complete. Nasser, looking worried, took me aside. "Abdullah and I have to show hard currency," he said. "Can you help us?" I hesitated, knowing that by any definition, assisting smugglers meant a two-year sentence, minimum, in a Turkish prison—and everyone knew the probable consequences, not counting time in a cell and a *persona non grata* passport stamp. I am not religious and hold few notions aside from human freedom and dignity sacrosanct. Both my freedom and dignity, however, were at risk. A long moment crawled by as I pondered consequences—an existential decision of crucial importance. Nasser's eyes flashed. "I won't steal it!" he said fiercely. "Of course not," I replied collecting myself and produced five twenty-dollar bills. "*Shokran,*" he uttered, and snatching the money, strode into the office with Abdullah, who was standing nearby.

Meanwhile, the driver revved the engine impatiently. I headed for the bus, mouth dry and breathing heavily, making it to the coach in time for departure. A moment later, my Palestinian brothers made safe haven close behind me. Passengers muttered in solidarity as we made our way down the aisle to the back of the bus. Our seats remained empty, and the contraband was undisturbed. *Another successful run for the Palestinian exiles,* I noted to myself, *but how many spins of the wheel remained?*

Comfortably seated, I felt more secure. Nasser leaned forward smiling; his right hand held the five bills, fanned like playing cards, which I plucked with relief. Nasser expressed his gratitude with the *bedu* formula: "We will meet again, *inshallah*." With all documents in order and the currency safe in my wallet, I savored the moment.

Antochia was located only a few miles from the Syrian border, and except for the delay, the dicey aspects of the trip were over, surely! A few miles past the Turkish frontier, the bus slowed, pulled to the right shoulder, and stopped. Just ahead, a military roadblock well protected by Turkish militia meant a thorough search for arms intended for Kurdish rebels; knowing official whim, however, I understood that any infraction might be enforced. My Palestinian companions shifted uneasily in their seats and whispered to one another.

A young soldier armed with a sidearm and an AK-47 boarded the bus. Standing in front with the attendant, he scanned the passengers. With my three-hundred-dollar down-filled winter jacket and Caucasian features, I looked decidedly out of place. The Turkish soldier conferred briefly with the steward and walked straight to the back, ignoring the rest of the passengers, who kept silent. He stopped at my seat and greeted me in Turkish, which I understood, but that single expression nearly exhausted my command of the language. I knew that Antochia was bilingual and hoped the young man had been reared locally. Heart's blood shaking, I spoke quickly with no thought for diction, pronunciation, syntax, or inflection. I included my name, age, and position at the university. I might have included the seminar titles and the required texts.

The soldier simply stared, entranced. I reached the end of my spiel and waited. An arrest would mean a thorough beating with no presumption of guilt or innocence. In the Republic of *Türkiye*, the procedure followed automatically, as a traditional feature of the booking process. Nothing personal; just policy.

Finally, the soldier grunted, made a crisp about-face, and exited the bus closely followed by the attendant. Presently, I heard the cargo door open, then slam shut. While the soldier returned to the barricade, the steward climbed aboard, and the engine started. With a lurch we regained the road, passed the barrier, and proceeded toward the city without further incident. A woman passenger sitting a few rows toward the front spoke privately to her husband, but my senses were heightened, and I overheard: "The American speaks Arabic well."

Stimulated by adrenalin, my preconscious had provided the right words along with the grammar and tonal stress in a moment of crisis. I savored the reward—a sense of freedom and well being—for temporary fluency: no arrest, no beating, no turn in the barrel courtesy of the notorious Turkish prison system. As a bonus, no negative comment from a native speaker for my usual substandard expression on all levels. On the contrary, the indirect praise for communicating well in Arabic, a difficult tongue for adult English speakers, was both rare and genuine. After several years in the Middle East, the overheard exchange served as a treasured confirmation of my stilted language skills.

After a long wait at the bus shelter, I felt relieved when Moodie arrived. We then took a cab to the Antioch terminal. Seated once again, I looked forward to the long, uncomfortable ride back, followed by a longer, well-earned rest in my own bed. We would then fulfill the pre-trip promise by arranging an *Iskender döner kebab* dinner for our friends and colleagues—some of whom had spent the *bayram* grading final exams and late assignments. Craftily, Moodie and I had turned in our grades early.

As generous sponsors of the feast, my Palestinian companion and I, bearing gifts, would entertain our guests and captive audience with exotic stories in the mode of "Gullible's Travels." I kept various receipts and official documents for the empirical proof; and if someone expressed skepticism at my Marco Polo tall tales, replied: "I'm Syrias."

XIV.

Back to the Boot

The double grief of a lost bliss is to recall its happy
hour in pain.—Dante

Over spring break at Łódz University, I invited Matthew Gibson to
join me on a trip to Italy, which I had greatly enjoyed when traveling through Europe after earning an MA in 1966. We arrived in
Palermo shortly after sunset and went by cab to a waterfront restaurant. Near the entrance, on a long wooden table, I noticed scores of
glistening mussels partially covered with brown seaweed and
smelling ocean fresh, like a day at the briny beach. "That's dinner!"
I announced as we entered. The meal exceeded my expectations, sec-
onded by Matthew. We gormandized until late on plump mollusks
steamed in a savory wine and garlic sauce served with a round peasant loaf slathered with hand-churned butter, helping ourselves to a
mixed salad with oil and vinegar. I preferred Chianti, but my more
knowledgeable friend opted for a fruity *pinot noir*. After several
rounds, the waiter approached. "*Dolce?*" Having noted a detail in
The Godfather after the turncoat driver's execution ("Leave the gun.
Take the cannolis."), we felt obliged to order the Sicilian pastry for
dessert.

As dedicated film *aficionados*, we regularly included favorite movie
dialogue in our conversations. Examples include: "We should have
shotguns for this kind of deal" (*Pulp Fiction*) upon entering the
Provost's office; "How much for everything?" (*Taxi Driver*) when considering several hundred dollars' worth of hand-rolled cigars at a
tobacco shop; and "She gave me the high hat" (*Miller's Crossing*),
when snubbed by the receptionist. My best contribution occurred one
night at a party, when I overheard a colleague mention Pavel Bosko,
an officious administrator, who had been summarily fired for insub-
ordination to the college President. "Oh. Paulie?" I interrupted. "You

won't see him no more," echoing Clemenza's reply when Sonny, the hot-tempered *capo*, enquired after Paul Gatto, the aforementioned treacherous driver.

After restful sleep in a one-night cheap hotel, we boarded a north-bound train, which was overcrowded, odorous, and uncomfortable. On returning from the cramped restroom, I found my seat occupied, which meant standing with several other passengers in the corridor for the remaining long hours. No one made eye contact or spoke. The ill-lit passenger car complemented physical discomfort on the morning express. None too soon we pulled into the Napoli station, wheels screeching in protest.

Retrieving luggage from overhead racks took considerable effort and athletic skill, as in basketball rebounds, which require elbow strikes and hip shots for maximum effect. Grunting, standing on my toes, I grabbed my battered Gladstone by the strap, yanked mightily until the bag swung free, and soon joined my companion on the platform. Matthew, who spoke fluent Italian, engaged in rapid conversation complemented by violent gestures for emphasis with a local tout, who had immediately identified us as foreign tourists. By happy coincidence, his *cugino* [cousin] offered accommodation—safe and at reasonable cost—nearby. As a bonus, he offered a free ride straight out of a Keystone Kops film short through the chaotic streets. Our newfound *amico* informed us that we could stash our luggage the next day when exploring the city and environs. *Ottimo!*

We bought a round-trip ticket for the train shuttle to Pompeii, a reasonably comfortable half-hour journey north of the city. After deboarding we stopped at a street vendor to sample gelato in an assortment of colors like a painter's palette. The emperor of ice cream, who spoke broken English, announced that several close relatives had emigrated to America and lived on Mott Street in lower Manhattan. "Know it well, and I loved the restaurants in little Italy when I worked on nearby Varick Street years ago," I said. He was delighted— "*Bravo!*"—and added a scoop of pistachio to the cone. During my twenty-five-year sojourn overseas, I often observed that beautiful

friendships were built on small gestures. As E.M. Forster stated succinctly: "Only connect."

We spent the day among the ancient, petrified ruins: a surreal experience, costing little. The volcanic eruption, which had occurred nearly
two thousand years ago, had spewed toxic smoke and ash, catching
the citizens unaware and freezing time: human bodies preserved at
the final moment for two millennia. Fascinated, we rarely spoke while
strolling about the city, which resembled a Hollywood set that belied
its genuine identity.

Upon leaving I noticed a pizza parlor. "According to one version of
culinary history," I announced, "the Romans invented the dish right
here. We've got to order a large pie with pepperoni." After a nearly perfect day of touring the frozen city, quoting at times from Bulwer-Lyt-
ton's *Last Days of Pompeii*, basking in the sunshine, admiring Mount
Vesuvius, the beautiful, still dangerous assassin—disappointment.
Defying expectation, the pizza proved decidedly mediocre: burned
crust, gummy mozzarella, soggy green peppers, briny meat slices,
awash in olive oil—each slippery swallow confirming the slang term
"sliders." We left a generous, undeserved tip and caught the evening
train to the hotel.

Rising early, we headed due north to Milan by express. Compared to
rail service from Palermo to Napoli, the new, well-appointed train
offered a sense of luxury. We relaxed and dozed in the half-full car-
riage with comfortable seats; vendors provided refreshments featuring
Italian espresso and pastry. Upon arrival Matthew made arrangements
at the Hotel Grande, which was conveniently located and included a
dining room. "I don't know about this place," I joked. "We're a bit
young to check out of the Grand Hotel next week." My friend, twenty-
eight years my junior, chuckled in appreciation. "Let's eat first and
walk to the square up the street afterwards."

Seated at a small table with starched napkins and heavy flatware, I
ordered *spaghetti allo scoglio* [pasta with seafood] and garden salad.
Matthew chose crab-stuffed ravioli and chicken cacciatore with wine

sauce. The waiter placed a carafe of dry *Frascati* within reach. We ate heartily and toasted absent friends. "Just loving this trip," I announced with genuine enthusiasm. "No matter what," I quoted, "we'll always have Milano." My film-savvy friend grinned in appreciation.

Milano was a city of contrasts: a thriving population center, the fifth largest in Italy, famous for fashion design, industry, and commerce while preserving Roman monuments throughout the metropolis. Upscale clothing stores, beautifully maintained parks, relics of the past—all were located within walking distance of our hotel. "We have both seen enough medieval sanctuaries to last a lifetime and beyond," I said, "but we should at least take a closer look at the Milan Cathedral. As you know, the architecture is often featured in documentaries, and pictures are standard, color plates in coffee table books."

The Duomo commanded the plaza and surroundings. In its actual presence, even non-believers were momentarily stunned. Like the fairytale castle—a symphony of hand-carved stone—multiple spires stretched to the heavens, reducing human stature and self-importance. "The better to understand 'finite,' " I observed. "Right," Matthew agreed, "I grew up in Salisbury with its famous cathedral and I've seen Notre Dame a few times, but this basilica has no equal. I haven't thought of the apostolic succession since public school, but I may review the matter," he said half seriously. "Let's explore the Galleria."

Entering the spacious arcade, I recalled Walter Benjamin's *flâneur* and behaved accordingly: eyeing store fronts, wandering without purpose, observing the spectacle. Milano's huge shopping mall, built in 1861, had served shoppers, tourists, and young people on the make. Comparing the protocols of 1966, I immediately noticed a difference in the courting ritual: no evidence of the stern chaperone, who for centuries had kept the putative virgins under hawk-like surveillance, ensuring that eligible young ladies preserved their innocence until the wedding night. Prospective lovers dressed in their finery now promenaded like peacocks, alert for the slightest sign of approval. The women wore peasant blouses (the better to display bounteous bosoms) complemented by tight, polished-cotton skirts that accentuated hips and cheeks. Glancing shyly, their bee-stung lips like cherries, slightly parted, there was a hint of a coy smile. Marble statures could not ignore the tempting nymphets. Countless generations had depended on the provocative strolls through the mall. We loafed for hours and promised a return to Milano's stadium as avid fans of the city's spectator sport.

Toward the end of the week sightseeing, complemented by savory snacks, souvenir hunting, and lively conversations, a highlight for me occurred while admiring a Roman arch straddling a well-traveled road in downtown Milan. Classical artifacts, unlike modern structures, were built to last and tended to survive fire, flood, vandals, and bombs. We noted that the flashy Ferraris, Fiats, Lancias, and occasional Lamborghinis passing under the arch were speeding to the junkyard, just a matter of decades in most cases, while the sturdy ruin would likely survive us both throughout the millennium. By chance, I turned to note a show window and felt a surge of nostalgia: presentation-grade Italian picklock stilettos and a variety custom switchblades. As in a movie flashback, I had beheld similar folders stuck in large cork globes featured in souvenir shop windows along Forty Second Street in the 1950s. Again, I now felt momentarily transfixed, captured by the past. Out of breath, heart pounding, I said, "Catch you later for chow. Got to check out the knives," and hurried to the cutlery store.

Inside I quickly found the pocket-folder display and, in regressive mode, gazed at the picklocks, clasp knives, Texas toothpicks, and front openers arranged side by side, some bone-handled with engraved bolsters and a leather thong at the butt end. While gazing at the shiny and well-honed bayonet, Wharncliffe, drop point, Persian, and spear blades, a helpful clerk speaking English opened the glass cabinet with a small key and placed several high-end knives on the counter. "Do you prefer leaf or coil spring?" he asked. "So long as it makes a good kick," I replied.

I chose a custom-made stiletto, released the locking mechanism, and pressed the blade into the handle. I immediately noticed the fit and finish: much superior to the 1950s model, including the more expensive Hoffritz automatic knives at the Port Authority Building. I pressed the large silver button, and the steel snapped into place, jolting my wrist. "Nice piece," I said. "My first picklock cost me $8.99 in New York over fifty years ago." "Prices have gone up," the young man replied. "With the strong dollar, we can ship it home for under a hundred euros." I replaced the knife and said, "Well, I work overseas and won't be returning to the States for awhile. Just looking." The young man said pleasantly, "Take your time." I did and, after examining the handmade automatics, headed back to the hotel for the evening feast.

Over a secular last supper, I recalled the infamous porno film *Debbie Does Dallas*, which I missed at the time, but had always found the title amusing. Borrowing the idiom I announced: "Well, I guess we have "done" Milano. Let's not overstay our welcome." Matthew responded that he was way ahead of me; in fact, he had called the airport and booked a flight for early the following morning. At dawn after checking out, I exclaimed "Cioa" to all within hearing range as we exited the hotel, luggage in hand and fond memories of our stay.

XV.

End Notes

And, now that life had so much promise in it, they resolved to go back to their own land; because the years, after all, have a kind of emptiness, when we spend too many of them on a foreign shore.

—Nathaniel Hawthorne

In retirement, I went on living in the village of Crestwood Farms, a suburb of Richmond, distant from family and friends, who reside all over the map. Solvent, in good health, and content, I kept in touch through correspondence and phone calls, plus made occasional short trips to pay the old surprise visit. At home, where I spent most days, I largely occupied myself by training, reading, and editing manuscripts—though given my advanced age and limited attention span, the stay-at-home activities fell short, leaving me a surplus of time. To overcome chronic boredom, I wrote a number of scholarly articles, without much success: just one conference presentation followed by a published essay. The unsung gems languish in the drawer.

I avoid clichés but soon understood that given my employment history, overseas adventures, and current circumstances, I was virtually obliged to write my memoirs—which carry the connotation of a valedictory address for those who will survive me. I resist that reading and looked for a remedy, always close at hand: literature. Unlike Don Quixote, Emma Bovary, Roskolnikov, et al., I have never been undone by consulting books. Quite the reverse. At this existential crisis, I again invoked Nabokov's *Pale Fire* narrator Dr. Kinbote, the supreme scholar-antihero and thorough professional failure as disgraced manuscript thief, inept editor, and scorned colleague. Yet despite his alarming mental state and unlimited capacity to misread an unchallenging text,

Kinbote finally understood the poem he virtually rewrote to fit his delusional fixation as Charles the Beloved, prince in exile.

Thus, "I was the shadow of the waxwing slain/By the false azure in the windowpane;/I was the smudge of ashen fluff—and I/Lived on, flew on in the reflected sky." The first lines of "Pale Fire" establish the theme of death and the remote possibility of shadowy flight beyond human existence, which is by all accounts notoriously short. As Beckett expressed the scandal of human brevity, we "give birth astride the grave."

Toward the conclusion of the novel in the unlikely form of an extended commentary on the poem, Professor Kinbote assured the imagined ideal reader, counter-intuitively sympathetic to his plight, that he "will rid myself of any desire" to end his days by self-destruction. Rather, like the slain waxwing's avian double, he would live on in a reflected, changed avatar—as "life is short and art long":

> I shall continue to exist. I may assume other guises, other forms, but I shall try to exist. I may turn up yet, on another campus, as an old, happy, healthy, hetero-sexual Russian, a writer in exile, sans fame, sans future, sans audience, sans anything but his art.[3]

For me, no academic encores are likely, nor are fame and celebrity (which I loathe) foreshadowed in the final act. However, if a select few readers find my accounts amusing, provocative, and/or similar to their own experience, I, too, shall continue to exist—and in a wholly satisfactory manner.

---

[3] Nabokov, Vladimir, *Pale Fire* (New York: Vintage International Edition, 1989), 300-01.

Lightning Source UK Ltd.
Milton Keynes UK
UKOW01f0036250616

277034UK00001B/139/P